The technique of
MACRAMÉ

This book is dedicated to my parents,
Maynard Burleson and Elizabeth Garner Burleson

The technique of MACRAMÉ

BONNY SCHMID-BURLESON

B T BATSFORD LIMITED   LONDON
CHARLES T BRANFORD COMPANY
NEWTON CENTRE   MASSACHUSETTS

Acknowledgment

I wish to thank all the artists who contributed photographs or allowed us to photograph their work. It is their skill in knotting and their willingness to share it with others that has enabled me to assemble this exceptional collection of macramé.

I especially wish to thank the following artists and friends for the kindness and hospitality shown us as we travelled through the United States photographing macramé: Dorris Akers, Jean Battles, Ron Franks, Joan Michaels Paque, Marianne S. Rodwell, Evelyn Söllner-Reid, Jon Wahling and Barbara Wittenberg.

Above all, I thank my husband, Claus-Peter Schmid for his excellent photography and drawings, his active support and encouragement.

Bonny Schmid-Burleson 1974

© Bonny Schmid-Burleson 1974
First published 1974
ISBN 0 7134 2520 2

Library of Congress Cataloguing in Publication Data
Schmid-Burleson, Bonny
The Technique of Macramé
Includes bibliographies.
1 Macramé.   1 Title.
TT840.S36   746.4   73–17335
ISBN 0-8231-7034-9

All photographs and drawings by Claus-Peter Schmid,
unless otherwise indicated.
Designed by Charlotte Baron, Libra Studios
Filmset in Monophoto Garamond, 11 on 13 point
by Servis Filmsetting Ltd, Manchester
Printed in Great Britain
by Wm Clowes & Son Ltd, Beccles, Suffolk
for the publishers
B T Batsford Ltd, 4 Fitzhardinge Street, London W1H 0AH
and Charles T Branford Company
Newton Centre, Massachusetts

Contents

Introduction

Recent years have seen a great revival of interest in hand crafts and especially textile crafts. Among these, macramé is gaining increasing importance. It offers the opportunity to explore various fibres as they are combined into an immense array of forms and designs, whether traditional or free-form, by the arrangement of elementary knots. This book on macramé and knotting has been written with a twofold purpose. First to introduce the beginner to the basic techniques of knotting, and to offer to the advanced artist further techniques in the form of elaborate patterns and braids. Chapters 1 to 4 concern themselves primarily with various techniques and examples of macramé. Secondly, the intention of this book is to demonstrate the potential of knotting as an art form. Chapters 5 to 9 examine the many possibilities of advanced macramé using the basic knots, Cavandoli technique, macramé incorporating other objects, macramé with other crafts, and the knotted structure. Chapter 10 shows many knotted variations on one theme, the mask. The illustrations throughout the book include some of the best and most original macramé work being done today. With the exception of one sampler, there are no directions given to these examples. Rather, it is hoped that they will inspire the reader to explore the artistic possibilities inherent in knotting.

1 Materials, equipment, designing and measuring

1 *(opposite)* *Primitif,* 135 cm × 80 cm
(4 ft 5 in. × 2 ft 7 in.), Marianne S. Rodwell.
Natural hemp, mounted on wood,
supports handmade ceramic beads and
masks

MATERIALS

Macramé is the art of tying strands of various fibres into a variety of designs and patterns for practical or aesthetic purposes. Of prime consideration to the knotter is the selection of the proper fibre or cord. Although an experienced knotter can tie practically any cord into macramé knots, there are some types which are especially suitable for macramé work. In general, the best cords are firm and evenly twisted or braided. Braided cords resist the stress of knotting very well, whereas care must be taken in the selection of twisted cords to ensure that they are indeed very firmly twisted.

The twist of a cord is an important consideration in the design of a macramé piece. Figure 76 is an excellent example of a piece where the strong twist of a cord is used to great advantage. A cord which has a strong structural pattern from its twists is better suited for use in a simpler knotting pattern where this structural quality can be shown off. The effectiveness of this principle is obvious in figure 76 as the stark simplicity of the knot contrasts with the highly structured rope. On the other hand, a cord with a less obvious structure, such as is the case with most braided cords, is ideal for a more complicated pattern where the intricacies of the knots is the important element.

The term 'ply' refers to the number of strands that are twisted in a cord. A three-ply cord is a cord twisted from three strands as in figure 2. Ply, however, has no relation to the size of a cord which is usually described in terms of the diameter. Any size cord, from the very finest embroidery thread to the coarsest rope, can be knotted into macramé.

2 *(above)*   3-ply twisted cord
3 *(below)*   Braided cord

Naturally, cord size selection depends on the size of the final article. The mobile section in figure 4, being very small and delicate, was knotted in very fine embroidery thread. For a massive piece, as shown in figure 5, a heavy piping cord was selected. The inexperienced knotter is advised not to attempt work either too small or extremely large until more experience is gained; that is the time to explore the possibilities offered by work in unusual dimensions. With very fine cords, the work progresses slowly and the knots are difficult to see; in large scale work it is easy to lose the overall perspective.

Cord fibres are either natural or man-made or sometimes a combination. Among the commonly used natural fibres are cotton, flax (linen), wool, sisal, hemp and jute. Nylon, rayon, polypropylene and polyethylene are man-made fibres often used in macramé cord. Natural fibres, having a rougher texture, are easier to knot as the knots, once tied, will not easily loosen. Knots tied in man-made fibres often have the tendency to slip. Natural fibres are also often preferred because of their organic quality and interesting texture.

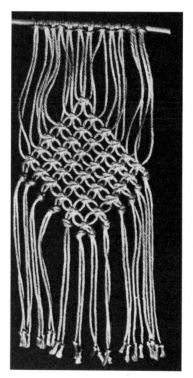 

4 *(left)* Detail of mobile, 12 cm × 4 cm (4¾ in. × 1½ in.), Bonny Schmid-Burleson. Tiny pattern of alternating flat knots and overhand knots in orange embroidery cotton, mounted on small piece of orangewood

5 *(right)* *Chinese Cloud,* 125 cm × 90 cm (4 ft × 3 ft), Francoise Grossen. Large construction in white piping cord. *Photo Tom Crane*

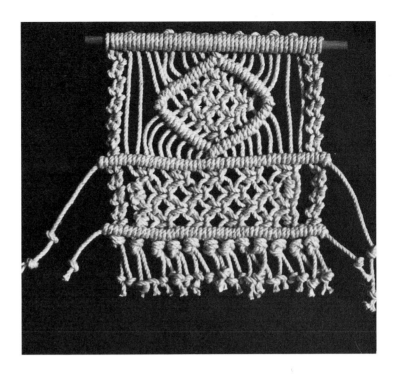

6 Sampler knotted in number 36 white cotton seine twine

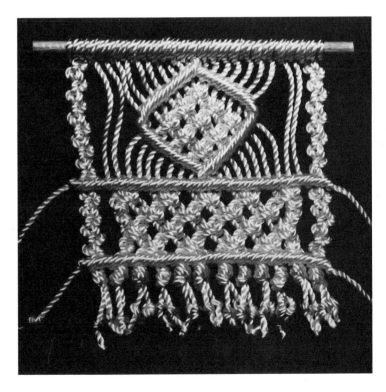

7 Sampler knotted in number 36 white nylon seine twine

The practicality of a particular fibre is also a deciding factor. Cords for belts should be strong and firm, whereas cord used in a wall hanging need not bear any stress other than being knotted, and hence may be more fragile if desired.

Knitting and rug wools and embroidery thread offer the widest range of colours but may not always be suitable for a particular project. Cotton seine twine, nylon seine twine, hemp, jute and sisal cords all dye well and easily. As dyeing is so easy, lack of colour in a cord should not be a deterrent to purchasing it, but rather an impetus to dyeing it oneself and experimenting with new colour combinations.

A basic cord for macramé is cotton seine twine. It is a 3-ply cord, inexpensive, sturdy and dyes and knots well. It comes in a variety of sizes from the very fine number 3 to the heavy number 120. Its companion, nylon seine twine, has a shiny surface and although more difficult to knot, can be made into beautiful pieces when the knots are tied closely together. Figures 6 and 7 show identical samplers in number 36 cotton and nylon seine twine. A comparison of *Winter Ptarmigan* in figure 73 and the sampler in figure 72 will clearly show the contrast between these two basic cords. As the cords are identical in colour, twist and size, one can readily see how fibre content alone changes the total appearance of a knotted object.

Nylon seine twine is, like the cotton twine, inexpensive and sturdy. When dyed it has an elegant sheen and delicate tonal quality. Some of the other cords widely used are hemp cords, jute, crochet, cotton, dreadknot cord, sisal, linen, rug and knitting wools. Some experience is needed to learn how to handle the elasticity of knitting wools which can be a drawback in knotting. However, once their characteristics are well understood, they can be used and advantage taken of their wide colour range. For the beginner, rug wool is recommended as it is firmer. The creative knotter will not feel limited to just one cord in one piece, but will be interested in exploring the possibilities of combining several cords of various textures and sizes.

The hanging in figure 8 is particularly interesting as three different cords of different textures and sizes have been used, whereas the colour has remained constant.

8   Suspended hanging, 160 cm (5 ft 3 in.) long, Barbara Wittenberg. Textural interest created by contrast of white cords of different dimensions and fibres

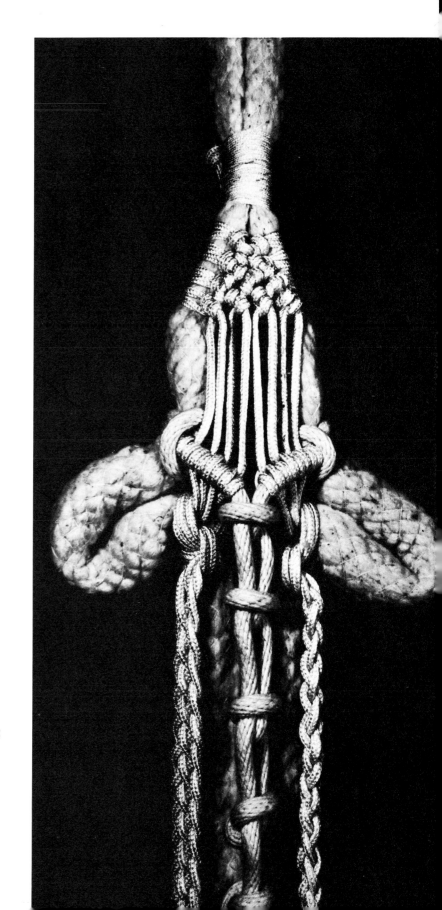

9 Suspended hanging *(detail)*, Barbara
Wittenberg. Matt surface of white piping
cord sets off shine of nylon cord. Cotton
cord adds third texture

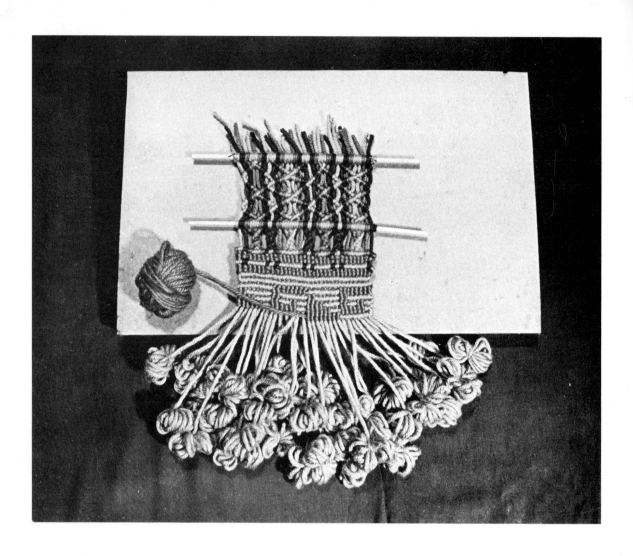

10 Unfinished piece mounted on foam
rubber knotting board. Ends tied in
bundles to facilitate handling

14

One of the great advantages of macramé is that relatively little equipment is necessary. The knotting itself is done by the hands without the aid of any special tools. However, as the work advances the knotter may wish to have more tools on hand, and is free to choose any equipment which is helpful to the craft. Few tools are made for macramé alone, but the equipment from other textile crafts such as weaving or crochet are often useful for macramé work.

One piece of important equipment is the knotting surface. There are perhaps as many different types of knotting boards as there are knotters. The essential thing is to devise a board where work can be held in progress and the knotter can work comfortably. Many knotters find foam rubber the most effective agent and keep various sizes available for use in different projects. Figure 10 shows a piece half finished as it is pinned on a foam rubber board. As the work progresses the completed knotting will be rolled up and moved up the board. The knotting board with the unfinished fringe in figure 11 is estimated as fifty years old. Here the knotter nailed the horizontal carrying cords to a wooden board. A piece of velvet provided a cushioned background.

Some people prefer to do large hanging pieces as they hang rather than pin them to a board. Other possibilities include a cork board mounted on a wall, carrying cords strung between two chairs or clamps mounted on a table or chair.

Other necessary equipment includes scissors, a tape measure and T or U pins to hold the piece to the knotting surface if it is to be secured. There is also an assortment of other small equipment which it is advisable to have. Crochet hooks are helpful in threading ends back into a knotted fabric. A collection of large-eyed needles is extremely useful for jobs such as stringing beads, tying ends back, weaving small sections by hand and sewing together pieces such as in a handbag. Rubber bands can be used to tie long working ends into bundles (figure 10). Clamps are useful in measuring off cords or holding down carrying cords for a suspended knotting surface. A warping rack such as used by weavers may be necessary in measuring and cutting extremely long strands.

The artist who dyes fibres will need a large dye pot and drying rack to dry the cords after they have been dyed.

11 Macramé fringe of unknown date, mounted on original wooden knotting board. Nails hold carrying cords on sides. Black velvet forms cushion under knotting. *Author's collection*

Plate 1 Mixed-media hanging, 110 cm × 70 cm (3 ft 7 in. × 2 ft 5 in.), Evelyn Söllner-Reid. Hanging of great tactile and textural interest. White wool roving, knitting wools and jute define each other as they contrast in texture and colour. Roving has been hooked to form top area of depth and softness. Half knot sennits help to suspend body of piece from brass rod mounting. Of central interest is the large wrapped flat knot

16

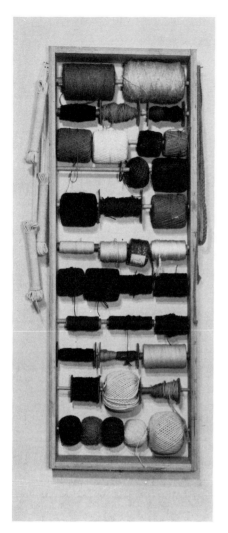

When one begins to do macramé on a larger scale, making pieces for sale or exhibition, more equipment to help in organization may become necessary. A well organized work area, equipment and records are great time and work savers in knotting. The knotter who has to spend time looking for a certain cord put away 'somewhere' or refiguring the measurements for similar items has naturally less time to spend in the creative side of macramé.

To keep a large selection of cords within easy reach and visibility, a cord rack may be devised as in figure 12. This easily constructed frame may be either hung on the wall or free standing.

A method of organizing beads, dowels and other items either found (sea shells, metal, feathers) or purchased (rings, buckles) should be worked out. Small jars are often best for beads and other small items, as the contents can be seen at a glance. Divided drawers may also help in organizing and storing.

A note book is very useful for cord and dye samples. Each time a new cord is purchased small samplers should be made and entered into a suitable note book. Name, cost, size, suitability and place of purchase may all be noted for easy reference (figure 13). A similar note book should also be kept for entering dye samples. Whenever a new colour is used or mixed, samples of different types of cords are dyed and mounted on a page. If the dye mixture is carefully noted it will not be difficult to achieve that tone again, and one has a ready reference to the effect of a particular colour on the different types of cords. It should be noted however that the cord should be dyed together for one piece. To repeat a colour tone exactly is almost impossible. The record of dye samples is helpful when the same colour is desired for a different piece.

12   Wall-mounted rack for cords. Dowels slide through on one side. Nails along outside provide extra hanging space

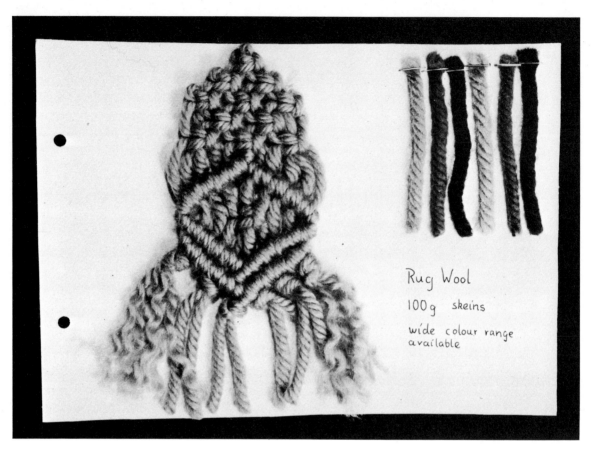

Rug Wool
100g skeins
wide colour range
available

13   Page from notebook of cord samples

The artist involved in large scale macramé work will find it helpful and time saving to keep careful records of past work; types of cord used, pattern and so forth. A small file box with cards is perhaps the best method of keeping track of projects. The design, length, type of cord and final size of piece can all be noted here. Later, when a similar piece is to be made, the card is there for reference. Well kept records of past work are a tremendous asset in designing and estimating material needs for present work.

Whether or not to plan the design of a macramé piece before the actual knotting begins depends on the artist. Many simply begin a piece and let the knotting follow their hands until completion. Françoise Grossen says 'It happens mostly in my head and then with my heart and fingers'. Some artists think out a piece thoroughly in advance of the knotting. They do not record these thoughts on paper, but rather follow the pattern in their mind. Joan Michaels Paque made preliminary sketches to *Levels of Consciousness* to visualize better the concept before the actual knotting of the construction. The hanging in figure 14 was planned in detail before its execution.

Generally, the more experience one has, the freer one can be about planning. The beginner may prefer to plan if for no other reason than to ensure the right amount of material. Planning should not be thought of as a hard and fast contract made with an idea. As the work progresses, the artist may find it necessary to change and improvise upon the original plan. Indeed, the final result may be quite different from the original sketch.

The amount of cord needed is something best learned from experience. As a basic rule it can be said that the thicker the cord, or the denser the knotting, the more cord is originally needed. For moderate denseness, approximately four times the finished length is required. If the cord is to be mounted double, as it usually is, eight times the final length should be cut. So if a wall hanging is to measure 50 cm (20 in.) and the cords are to be mounted double on a dowel, the individual cords should be cut 4 m (13 ft 4 in.) each.

There are exceptions to this rule. Obviously, a carrying cord which is not knotted itself will have a very slight take-up, about 10 per cent. Hence, when working rows of flat or half-knots, called sennits, the inside carrying cords only need to be about 10 per cent longer than the finished item. Working cords of the sennit should be about six times the finished length.

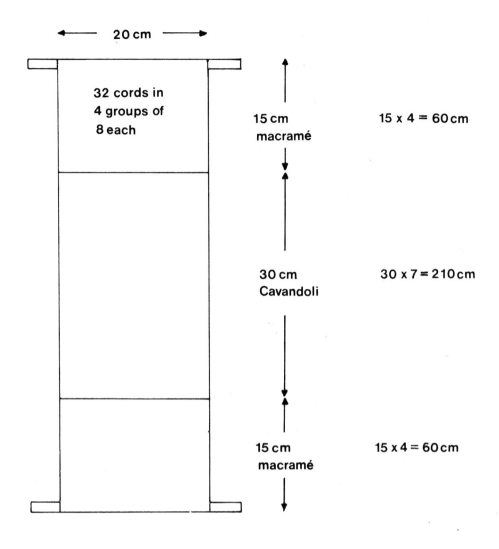

20 cm

32 cords in
4 groups of
8 each

15 cm
macramé

15 x 4 = 60 cm

30 cm
Cavandoli

30 x 7 = 210 cm

15 cm
macramé

15 x 4 = 60 cm

60
210
60
10 for mounting
10 for ending
_____
Total length of each strand: 350 cm

14 *(opposite)* *Steps to the Temple,* 60 cm × 20 cm (2 ft × 8 in.), Bonny Schmid-Burleson. Hanging in red, green and yellow rug wool. Central area is densely-knotted pattern in Cavandoli. Top and bottom sections are macramé. *Collection of Maynard and Elizabeth Burleson*

15 Design sketch for *Steps to the Temple,* showing calculation for cord lengths

When working a new, unfamiliar cord, it is advisable first to work a small sampler to determine just what the take-up will be. When the knotting is very dense, the amount of cord needed is greater. Cavandoli, which is the densest of all knotting, has an average take-up of seven times. If the cords are taken double, it is necessary to figure fourteen times the final desired length.

When working very large pieces, this considerable length can be quite cumbersome. These long ends may be tied into butterfly bundles, tied on small bobbins or wrapped into bundles held with rubber bands. In tying bundles with rubber bands, the wrapping should begin at a point close to the knotting and not the end of the cord. This way a simple pull on the bundle will lengthen the cord.

Figure 15 demonstrates the original sketches for the wall hanging in figure 14. The top and bottom are macramé, the centre section Cavandoli. When a piece such as this is carefully planned the cords can be cut to almost their exact lengths if the calculations for macramé and Cavandoli are made. The two different densities are taken into consideration in the planning. It should be noted that the cords have been mounted singly to allow for the fringe along the top. When the cords are mounted double as they very often are, half as many cords would be cut at twice the length. This particular wall hanging lends itself well to careful planning as it is geometric and relatively static. A free form piece is more difficult to plan and is also likely to be the piece that flows from the artist's hands at the time of knotting.

2 The basic knots

There are only three types of knots which are essential to macramé: the double half hitch, the flat knot and the overhand knot. The simple half hitch and half knot, also used extensively, are variations of the double half hitch and flat knot respectively. Other more elaborate knots may be easily integrated into macramé work but are not considered basic to the craft.

THE OVERHAND KNOT

The overhand knot is the simplest knot in macramé. It is tied with one length. In its most elementary form, a loop is made in the cord, one end pulled through the loop and tightened (figure 16). There are several variations possible with the overhand knot when tied in combination with other cords. Figures 17, 18 and 19 demonstrate methods of tying three different possible combinations. These knot combinations may then be alternated to create a net-like appearance. The sampler in figure 20 is knotted in alternating overhand knot patterns.

The overhand knot has both decorative and practical uses. It serves to tie off ends to prevent the cord from unravelling as well as to hold small items such as beads, shells or pebbles in place. The knot can look attractive when used to decorate cord endings or to accent areas of free hanging cord. In *Ritualis Number I* (figure 100), what would be a section of free hanging cords is given additional textural interest by the effective use of overhand knots and braiding.

16   Overhand knot tied in single cord

17 *(right)*   Overhand knot tied in single cord over another cord

18 *(far right)*   Overhand knot tied with two cords together

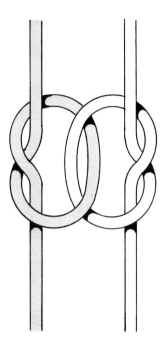

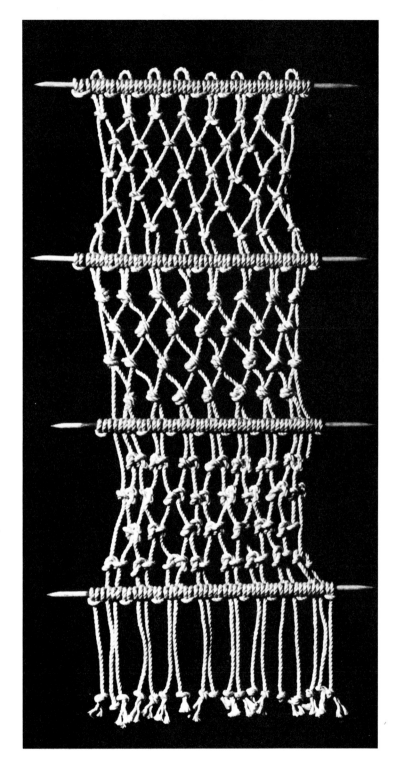

19 *(above)*   Two intertwined overhand knots

20 *(right)*   Sampler: nets made with overhand knots. From top to bottom: overhand knots tied with one strand over another in alternating fashion; overhand knots tied with two strands together in alternating fashion; intertwined overhand knots tied in alternating pattern

This is the most widely used and versatile of macramé knots. The first step in tying the double half hitch is made by looping one cord over another. This is the simple half hitch. The half hitch used alone is discussed in chapter 3 (figure 60). When the cord is looped the second time a tight knot is tied which is called the double half hitch, or cording when there is a row of such half hitches (see figure 21).

In tying double half hitches (as well as flat knots and half knots) it is necessary to distinguish between the cords which are knotted (knotting cords) and the cords which carry the knots (carrying cords). In double half hitching, the carrying cord is always placed over the knotting cord. The direction of a row of cording is decided by the direction of the carrying cord which holds the hitches. The carrying cord can be held horizontally, vertically or diagonally (figures 21, 22, 23, 25, 26). Areas of horizontal and vertical double half hitches create contrasting textural patterns as in figure 24.

21 *(left)* Horizontal double half hitch from left to right. Cord 2 is hitched over cord 1. Take care with the second hitch that the end of the cord is pulled through the space between the two hitches as shown. Cord 1, the carrying cord, must be held taut with the right hand while the left hand ties knot

22 *(right)* Horizontal double half hitch from right to left. Cord 1, the carrying cord, is held taut with the left hand while the right hand ties knot

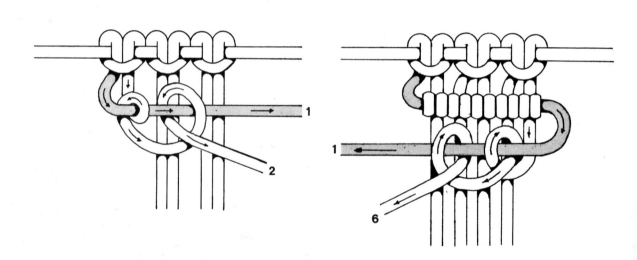

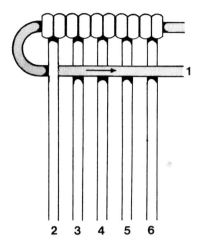 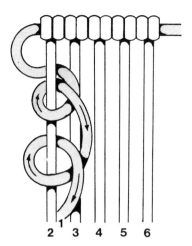 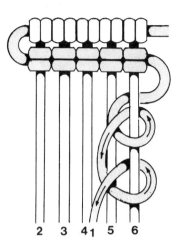

2	3	4	5	6

23 *(above)* Vertical double half hitches. From left to right: cord 1 is the knotting cord, cord 2 is the carrying cord, cord 1 is placed under cord 2; vertical double half hitch from left to right with cord 1 hitched over cord 2, right hand ties knot; vertical double half hitch from right to left with cord 1 hitched over cord 6, left hand ties knot. The row of vertical double half hitches from left to right is complete

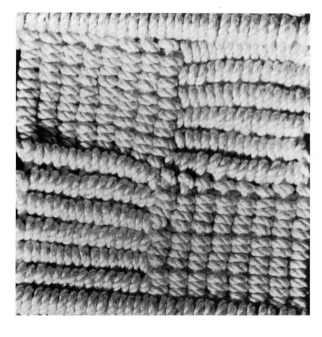

24 *(right)* Sampler: contrasting areas of vertical and horizontal double half hitches

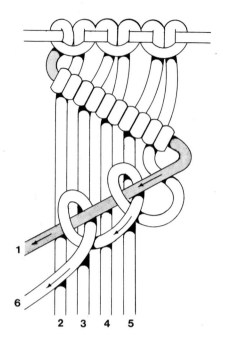

25 *(left)*   Diagonal double half hitch from left to right. Cord 2 is hitched over cord 1, the carrying cord. Cord 1 is held in the right hand while left hand ties knot

26 *(right)*   Diagonal double half hitch from right to left. Cord 6 is hitched over cord 1, the carrying cord. Cord 1 is held in the left hand while right hand ties knot

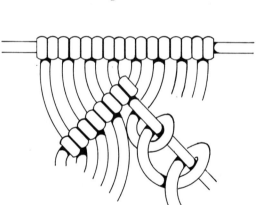

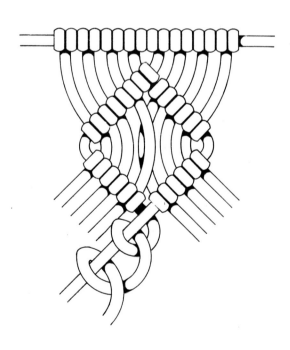

27 *(left)*   Diamond pattern knotted with diagonal double half hitches. Centre cords are hitched together and brought diagonally to outside

28 *(right)*   Completion of diamond. Cords brought back inside and hitched together

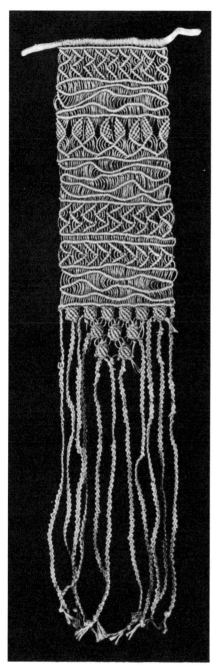

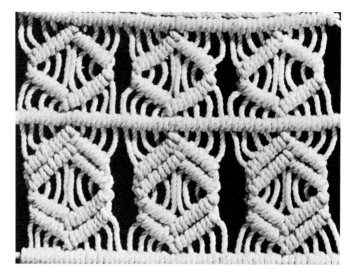

30 *(top)* Sampler: diamond pattern
made with diagonal double half hitches
with single and double borders

31 *(below)* Sampler: X pattern made
with diagonal double half hitches with
single and double rows

29 Wallhanging, Cathy Frank. Natural
linen cord knotted in double half hitches
shows the great variety possible with this
knot. Ends have been tied in half hitch
chains

Diagonal double half hitches are used in a myriad of designs
and patterns of which the popular diamond and X are just the
beginning (figures 30 and 31). The carrying cord may also be
moved in such a way to create rounded shapes or figurative
designs. The bird design in the hanging in figure 94 has been
developed by the free use of rows of double half hitching.

A half knot is one half of a flat knot. When two opposite half knots are tied the resultant knot is a flat knot. Flat knots and half knots are usually tied in groups of four, the two outside cords being tied over the two inside cords. However, the outside knotting cords may be several cords used as one over several carrying cords or over just one carrying cord, dowel or other type of carrier.

The method of tying the half knot is demonstrated in figure 32. Figure 33 shows three half knots in progress. When the half knot is repeated in this manner, the result is a spiral sennit (figure 34), a very attractive and widely used motif. The sennit will begin to twist at about the fourth knot. It is turned over and the knotting continued in this same manner.

32 *(left)* Half knot. Cord 4 is placed over carrying cords 2 and 3 and under the left hand cord 1. The left hand cord 1 is placed under carrying cords 2 and 3 and over the right hand cord 4. The cords are tightened. To continue, the cord now on the right (1) is placed over the carrying cords and under left hand cord 4. Cord 4 is brought under the carrying cords and over cord 1, bringing all cords back to their original position. This process is continued

33 *(right)* Three half knots in progress. When continued, this sennit will begin to twist after four knots

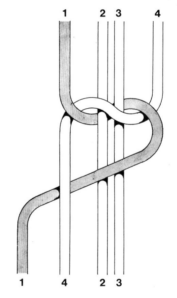

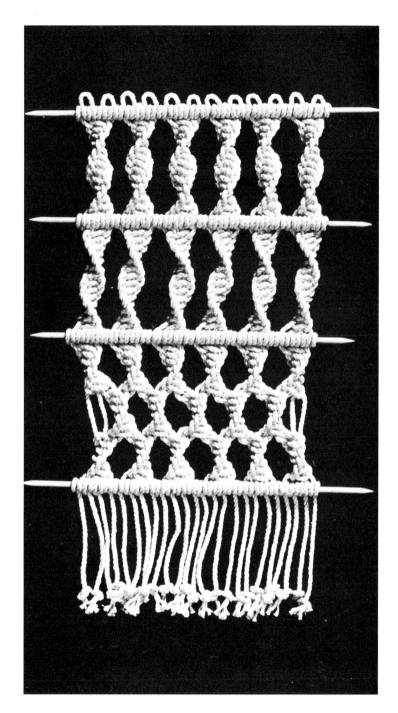

34 Sampler: half knot sennits. From top to bottom: half knot sennits formed with right hand half knots; half knot sennits formed with left hand half knots twisting in opposite direction; alternating half knot sennits, where sennits are knotted for one full twist of seven knots and then alternated by dropping first two cords in second row

35 Necklace *(detail)*, Jean Battles.
Sennits of half knots decorate area
between alternating flat knots and beads

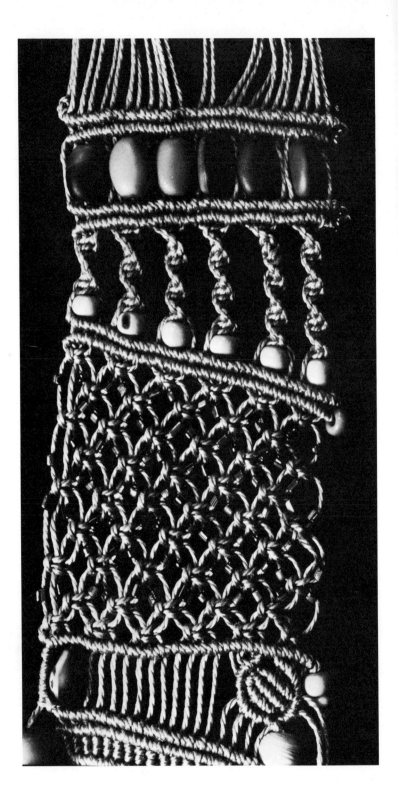

36 *(left)*   Start of flat knot knotted as half
knot

37 *(right)*   Flat knot. Second step
knotted as left hand half knot. Cord 1,
now on the right, is brought under
carrying cords 2 and 3 and then over cord
4. Cord 4 is brought over the carrying
cord (2 and 3) and under the loop formed
by cord 1, bringing all cords back to their
original position. The cords are
tightened

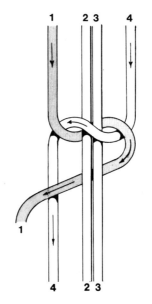
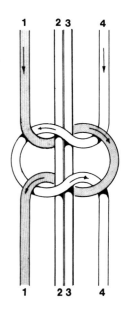

Plate 2   Necklace *(detail)*, Jean Battles

To tie a spiral sennit twisting in the opposite direction (figure
34), the method of tying the half knot is reversed. This pro-
gression may be seen in figure 37, this knot being the second step
to the flat knot. Here the right hand cord is placed under the
carrying cords and over the left hand cord.

Spiral sennits may be alternated (figure 34), or employed in a
variety of ways alone or in combination with other knots. The
hanging in figure 1 is composed primarily of spiral sennits.
Figure 35 is a detail from a necklace. Here the spiral sennits are
used to decorate one small area of a piece of knotted jewelry
which employs many different knot combinations. The necklace
may be seen in its entirety in figure 110.

The flat knot, often called the square knot, is a one-dimensional
knot; it does not twist but lies flat. It is formed by a combination
of the two opposite methods of tying the half knot. Figures 36
and 37 demonstrate the procedure for tying the flat knot. A
sequence of this knot results in a flat knot sennit (figure 38).
These in themselves may be used as the basis of a design or intertwined as in the sampler in figure 38.

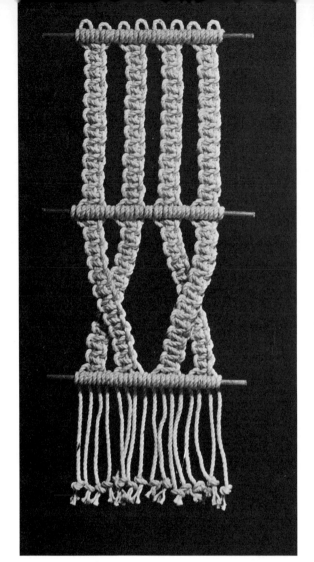
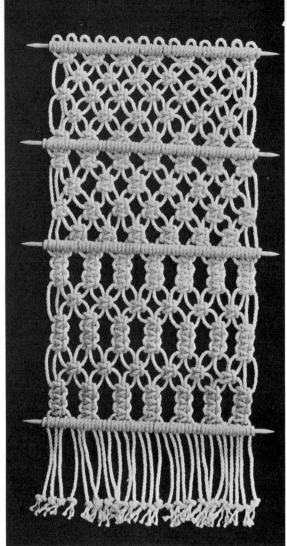

38 *(left)*   Sampler: flat knot sennits.
These are formed when the flat knot is
continued along the same carrying cords.
They may be exchanged as in sampler, to
form pattern

39 *(right)*   Sampler: patterns of
alternating flat knots. From top to
bottom: alternating single flat knots;
alternating triple knots (flat knot and one
half knot); sennits of three flat knots
alternated with single flat knots

34

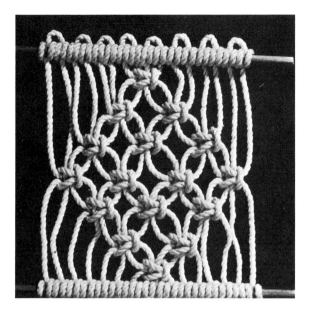

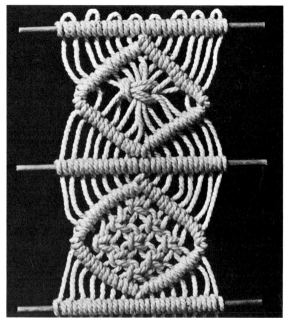

40 *(left)* Sampler: alternating flat knots
in natural diamond shape. By regularly
dropping or adding two cords in
alternating flat knots, diagonals are
formed as in this diamond

41 *(right)* Sampler: flat knots used to
decorate the inside of double half hitch
diamond

One of the most attractive and commonly used patterns is the
alternating flat knot pattern. To alternate flat knots, the two
outside cords on either side of a group of cords are dropped in
the second row. This procedure moves the knot two spaces so
that it is situated between and below the two knots above it,
forming an alternating pattern. Flat knots may be alternated
singly, in triple knots (flat knot plus one half knot) or any combination of flat knots (figure 39). Alternating flat knots provide
the central motif for the necklace in figure 42.

Single and alternating flat knots may also be used in combination with double half hitches as with the diamond pattern in
figure 41.

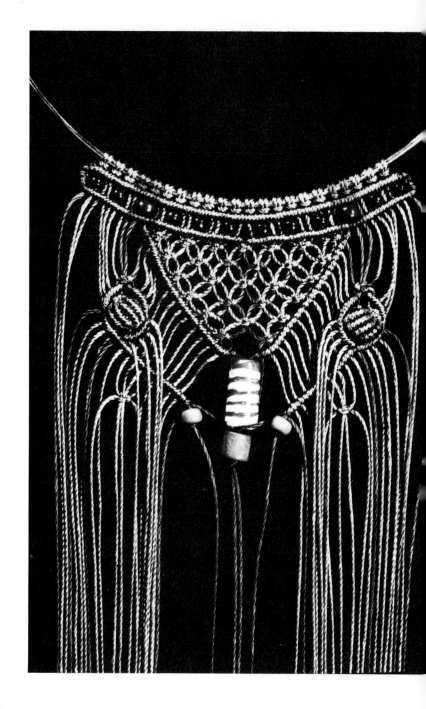

42   Necklace, Jean Battles. Upholstery
cord on silver neckpiece tied in
alternating flat knots and double half
hitches

3 More patterns, braids and fancy knots

43a *(above)* and 43b *(centre)* Alternating double half hitches. Each new row of hitches is tied from the opposite direction

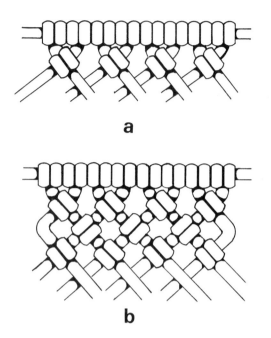

a

b

44 *(below)* Area of alternating double half hitches forms very dense, highly textured fabric

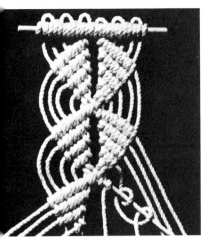
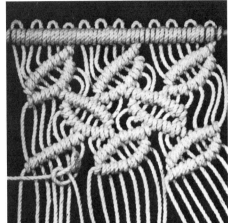
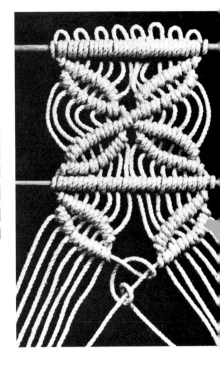

45 *(left)* Chevron pattern. Tied by continually bringing the innermost cords to the outside as carrying cords

46 *(centre)* Alternating leaf design formed with diagonal double half hitches. Leaf shape formed by holding carrying cord in slightly curved line

47 *(right)* Flower pattern formed by diagonal double half hitches. Four leaf shapes radiate from central point

MORE PATTERNS

The flat knot and double half hitch are the basic macramé knots. A basis of only two knots is not a limiting factor as might be assumed, as these two knots may be arranged in a seemingly infinite number of different patterns.

It would be virtually impossible to demonstrate all of the patterns. Their number is not only too great but knotters are continually developing new designs. The diamond and the X, elementary to macramé, were demonstrated in the preceding chapter. While not attempting to approach all patterns, this chapter illustrates some most frequently used. Only the flat knot button (figure 54) is tied with the flat knot, all others are double half hitch patterns. The berry (figure 51) and the hanging berry (figure 53) are particularly interesting in that they are three-dimensional units which may add texture and depth to a surface ordinarily flat. Noteworthy also are the leaf and flower patterns (figures 46 and 47). Here the carrying cord must be held in a curved line to form the leaf shape. This is the first step to figurative designing. A further elaboration of the leaf pattern and figurative knotting may be seen in the wall hanging in figure 94. The double half hitches have been knotted to create the image of a bird.

48   *Blue Flower,* 80 cm (2 ft 8 in.) long,
Bonny Schmid-Burleson. Hanging in dyed
blue hemp cord with white wooden beads
employs flower and leaf patterns.
Collection of Jurgen and Riki Suabedissen

40

49 Angling. One method of angling using horizontal and vertical double half hitches

50 Necklace, Jean Battles. Knotted in brown upholstery cord, featuring angling. Indian trade bead used as centre decoration.

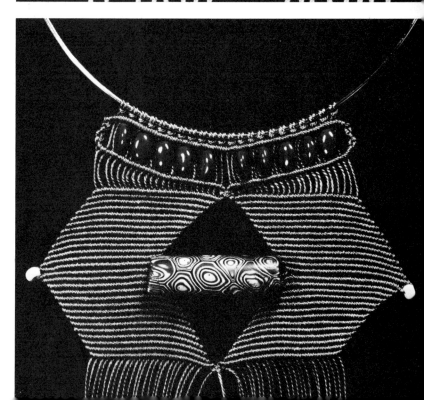

51 The berry knot. A small dimensional pattern tied with double half hitches. A minimum of eight cords needed. From left to right: two flat knots are tied as a base; four rows of diagonal double half hitches are tied by bringing the right hand cords over the left; flat knots are tied as the bottom base around the double half hitches, the hitches are then pushed outward from beneath

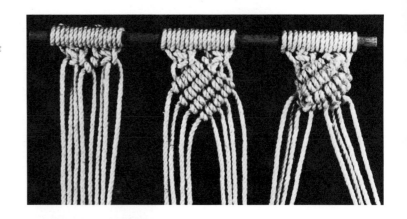

52 Wallhanging *(detail)*, Cathy Frank. Wallhanging in white cotton cord features berry knot

42

53 Hanging berry. Rounded shape formed by vertical double half hitches. Vertical cords are carrying cords for one long horizontal cord. With each turn, an increasing number of cords is used until the berry reaches its widest point. To narrow the berry, fewer cords are used until the berry reaches its final size. For wrapping, see figure 55

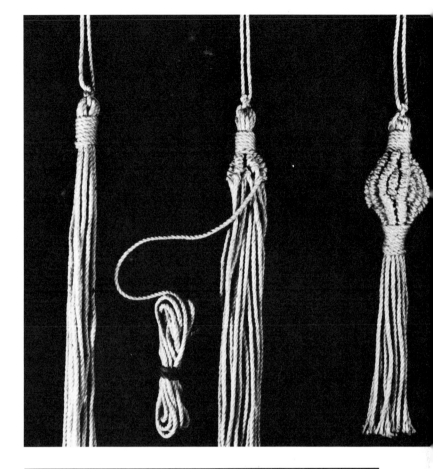

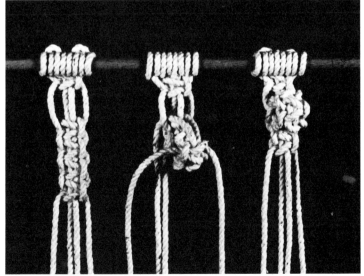

54 Flat knot button. The flat knot button is a flat knot sennit rolled over on itself once. A small sennit of four or five knots is tied, the end rolled up and around, the carrying cords being brought through the loops and back down. The sennit is then continued

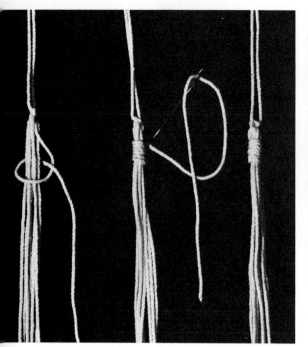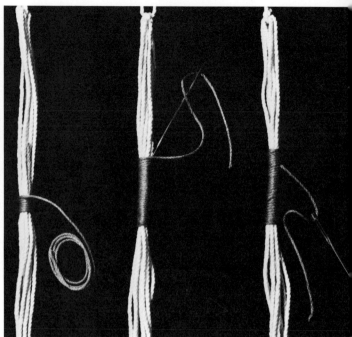

55 *(left)* Method of wrapping coil as for a small tassel. From left to right: gathering knot; cord is wrapped up from gathering knot and needle used to pull cord through coil; finished coil

56 *(right)* One method of wrapping. Embroidery cotton used to wrap cotton seine twine. From left to right: one end of embroidery cotton is wrapped under the coil; needle used to insert end of cotton into coil; needle exits several coils from the end, end of cotton will be trimmed

WRAPPING

Wrapping, although not traditionally considered as macramé, is used so widely in knotting that it must be recognized as an important element. Wrapping may perform a practical function such as tying off ends or forming a tassel (figure 55). In the hands of an inventive artist, it becomes a new means of artistic expression in fibres (figures 57 and 59).

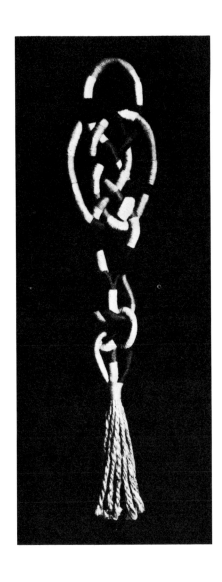

57 *(left)* Wrapped hanging, 1 m (3 ft 3 in.) long, Evelyn Söllner-Reid. Wrapped jute formed into oriental knot and flat knot. Bright red, blue and yellow knitting wools used to wrap natural jute.

58 *(right)* Wrapped hanging *(detail)*, Evelyn Söllner-Reid

8 strand square sennit

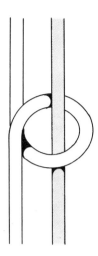

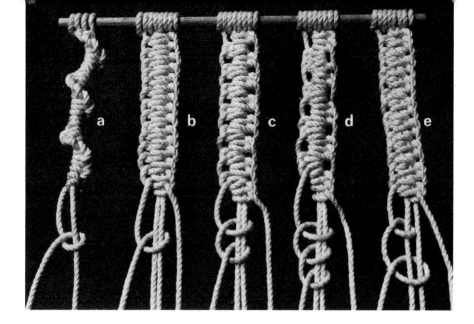

BRAIDING

Braids and sennits are an important complement to knotting.
Knotted braids may be used alone as in a belt; as a design
element in a larger piece, or intertwined and rearranged to form
new patterns.

The flat knot sennit and spiral sennit were introduced in
Chapter 2. These are only two of a great number of braids which
may be tied with macramé knots. Further braids may be knotted
using the simple half hitch and the reversed double half hitch.

The half hitch is one hitch or loop made with one cord around
another (figure 60). By itself it does not make a firm knot as does
the double half hitch. However, when worked in a series the
resultant braid is quite firm.

A half hitch spiral may be made by continually working half
hitches from one side over a carrier (figure 61). To make a half
hitch braid which lies flat the hitches should be worked from
alternating sides of a carrier. The simplest braid is worked by
hitching one cord first from the right and then from the left and
so on. This principle may be easily altered to form new braids.
Working two or three hitches from each side before alternating
changes the appearance of the braid.

47

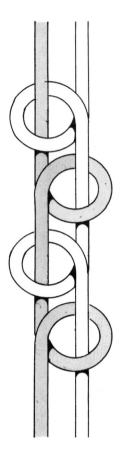

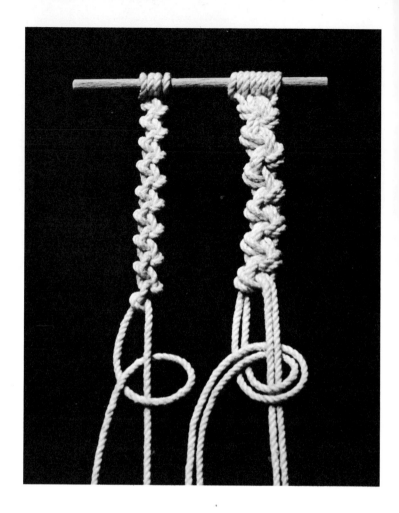

62 *(left)* Half hitch chaining. Tied in multiples of twos, a half hitch chain is formed by alternating hitching one cord over another

63 *(right)* Half hitch chaining formed by two strands and four strands

The half hitch is also used to make the half hitch chain, a versatile and easily made construction. Unlike the braids described above, the half hitch chain is not worked over a carrier, but each cord is hitched in alternating steps over the other (figure 62). The half hitch chain may be worked with two cords or a heavier chain can be made with four cords (figure 63).

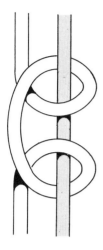

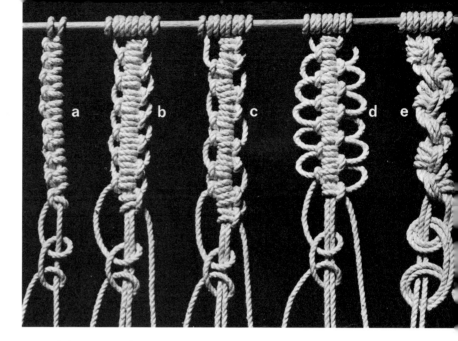

64 *(left)* Reversed double half hitch. This knot, like the double half hitch, consists of two half hitches. However, the second hitch is tied in the opposite manner to the first. The first hitch goes over and under while the second hitch is under and over

65 *(right above)* Braids tied with reversed double half hitches. From left to right: reversed double half hitches repeatedly tied from one side over another cord; the same tied from alternate sides over central carrying cords; two reversed double half hitches tied from alternate sides over central carrying cords; reversed double half hitches tied from alternate sides over carrying cords, loops made by tightening the knot below the braid and then sliding it into place; reversed double half hitch chain formed by alternating hitching one cord over another

66 *(right below)* Intertwined reversed double half hitches. Inside cords are alternately exchanged

The reversed double half hitch, like the double half hitch, is two half hitches. However, the second hitch is tied in the opposite way to the first. The first hitch goes over and under, while the second hitch is under and over (figure 64). Braids made with the reversed double half hitch are made over a carrier and are usually worked in groups of four cords (figure 65). A series of reversed double half hitches may be tied from one side or alternating sides. When working from alternating sides, it is possible to create variety by working two or three reversed double half hitches before changing sides (figure 65c). Extra decorative effects may be created by leaving more cord between the hitches to form loops (figure 65d) or by knotting two parallel braids and exchanging the inside cords (figure 66).

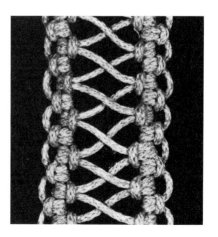

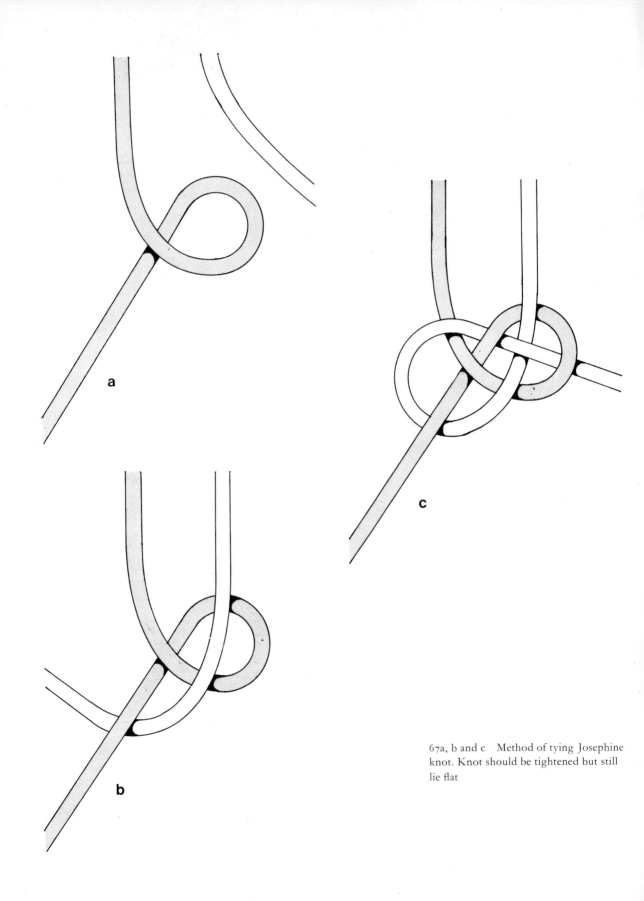

a

b

c

67a, b and c   Method of tying Josephine knot. Knot should be tightened but still lie flat

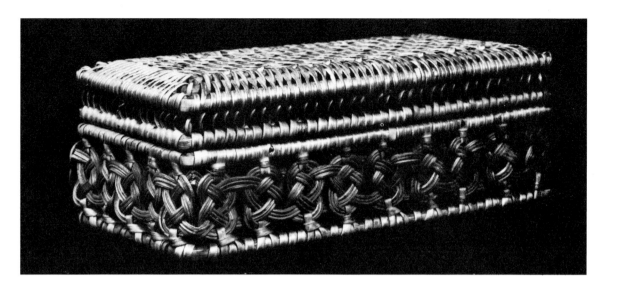

The half hitch, double half hitch, flat knot, half knot and over-hand knot are considered macramé knots. There are, however, many more elaborate knots which may be used in combination with the basic macramé knots, or may even be used alone to create an unusual knotted item. Some of these knots are familiar practical knots used in a new artistic context. Many are decorative knots of the Chinese or Japanese, people to whom knot tying has been and is a great art.

The method of tying two very popular knots, the Josephine and Chinese crown knot, are demonstrated in this chapter (figures 67a, b and c and 70 a and b). The reader will notice that many of the illustrated pieces contain interesting and unusual knots which are identified in the captions. As it is not the intention of this book to teach elaborate knot tying beyond the macramé knots, the reader is referred to *Ashley's Book of Knots* for almost four thousand different knots or to Paque's *Visual Instructional Macramé* for an excellent collection of knots particularly suitable to macramé work.

68 Woven straw box, 13 cm (5 in.) wide, 8 cm (3 in.) long. Josephine knots form outside band. *Collection Jon Wahling*

69 Necklace, Barbara Wittenberg.
Josephine knot is central motif for
striking necklace. Neckpiece supported
by flat knot sennit

52

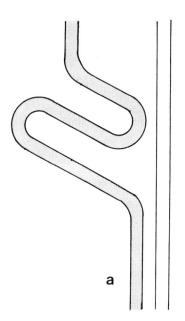 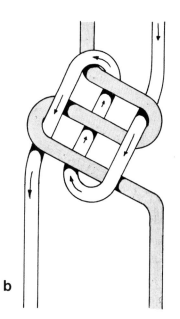

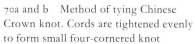

70a and b   Method of tying Chinese
Crown knot. Cords are tightened evenly
to form small four-cornered knot

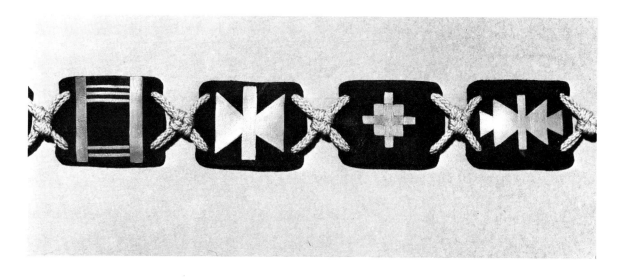

71   Belt, Bonny Schmid-Burleson. Small
sections of painted leather threaded on
braided cotton cord. Chinese crown knots
are tied between each leather unit

DIRECTIONS

Material   White seine twine

Cutting   Twenty-one strands, each 4 m (13 ft 3 in.) long, mounted double on dowel, making forty-two vertical working cords. Extra 8 m (26 ft 6 in.) of twine, cut into sections for horizontal rows

Knotting   Strands are divided into three sections of ten strands, each with four cords between each group for braiding

First row	Flat knot sennit—berry knot—half knot sennit—diamond pattern—half knot sennit (opposite direction)—chevron pattern—flat knot sennit
Second row	Single half hitch sennit—alternating leaf pattern—double half hitch sennit—flat knot buttons—triple half hitch sennit—overhand knots—half hitch sennit (first over one carrier and then over both)
Third row	Half hitch sennit (first over one carrier, then over both, finally over one again)—alternating flat knots—reversed double half hitch sennit—Chinese crown knot—double reversed double half hitch sennit
Fourth row	Reversed double half hitch sennit with loops—zig-zag—half hitch chain—X pattern—reversed double half hitch chain—interlaced reversed double half hitches—reversed double half hitch sennit from one side
Fifth row	Half hitch twist—Josephine knot—flat knot sennit with overhand knots—alternating half knot sennits—half hitch twist
Sixth row	Half hitch chaining—flower pattern—flat knot sennit—arrow formation of double half hitches—half hitch chaining
Seventh row	Half hitch chaining—diamond pattern with weaving—half hitch chaining

Overhand knots tie cords below last horizontal row and at ends of cords to prevent unravelling

72 *(opposite)* Sampler: an attractive wall hanging in white nylon seine twine. Recommended to beginners to learn the basic knots, patterns and braids as a future reference

The purpose of this chapter has been to describe some of the patterns and braids possible with macramé, along with two additional ornamental knots. The beginner will want to learn these patterns and braids as a thorough foundation in knotting techniques and patterns. It is suggested that the beginner make the sampler in figure 72, either as it is or with slight variation. It contains basic, classic macramé patterns and the Josephine and Chinese crown knots within the small sections. These are divided by the different braids described earlier. Apart from the valuable experience gained from knotting such a piece, the knotter will also have a permanent record of the knots and patterns, as well as an attractive wall hanging.

73 *Winter Ptarmigan (detail)*, Dorris Akers. Clear view of figure-eight knots and turk's heads. Small knot in centre of frame is wrapped in pink, being the only touch of colour in a totally white piece. It represents the heart of the soaring ptarmigan

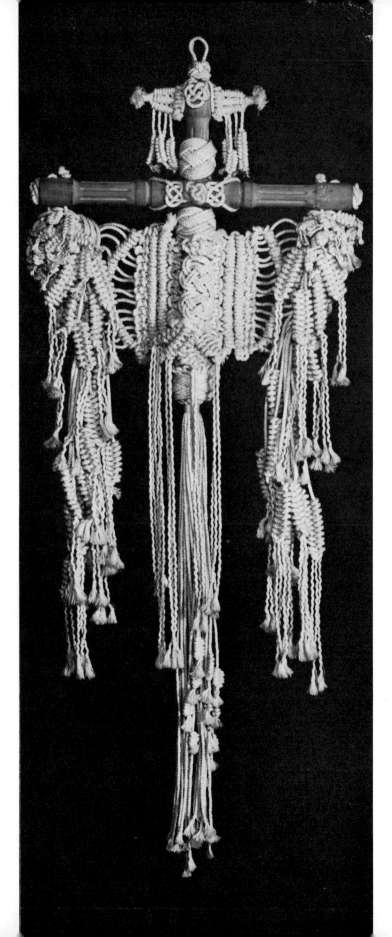

74 *Winter Ptarmigan.* 120 cm × 90 cm (4 ft × 3 ft), Dorris Akers. Extensive use of elaborate knots characterize this piece in white cotton seine twine on wooden frame. Josephine knots may be seen in the centre, while figure-eight knots are tied in the ends. Turk's heads and crown knots are also used

4 Mounting, finishing, replacing, and adding cords

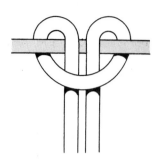

75   Reversed double half hitch as used in mounting

76   *Snug,* 90 cm × 40 cm (3 ft × 1 ft 4 in.), Dorris Akers. Reversed double half hitch in twisted 5 cm (2 in.) manilla rope, used as basic design element

MOUNTING

There are many methods of mounting cords onto a dowel, buckle or other type of carrier. They range from simple, functional mountings to elaborate, decorative ones. The easiest method of mounting cords is to use the reversed double half hitch or, as it is often called when used in this manner, the lark's head hitch. The cords are taken double and hitched onto the carrier as in figure 75. This mounting is also used to mount cords on fabric to make a macramé fringe. The simplicity of the lark's head makes a dramatic hanging in figure 76 where the knot alone is the central design motif.

Often a more elaborate mounting than the lark's head is called for. There are several methods available for decorative mountings. All are based on the double half hitch. The knotter may also create new mountings based on the principle of the double half hitch.

The basic procedure for the double half hitch mounting is to double the cord, place it under the carrier and then double half hitch each side of the cord to the carrier (figure 77). This mounting has the appearance of a row of cording (which it is) and the carrier is completely hidden from view. All decorative mountings are variations of this method. Before the second half of the cord or both ends are hitched to the carrier, something is done to the cord or cords to add a decoration. This may be in the nature of a loop (figure 77), overhand knot (figure 79), chaining (figure 81), flat knot (figure 83) or any combinations of these.

The detail of the handbag in figure 107 clearly shows a double half hitch mounting with one loop. Cords may be mounted singly, in twos or even in threes. It should be noted that the more cords that are used in a single mounting, the larger the total piece should be. The mounting must be proportional to the size of the finished knotted item.

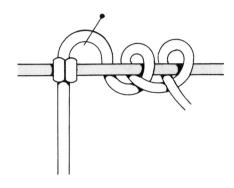

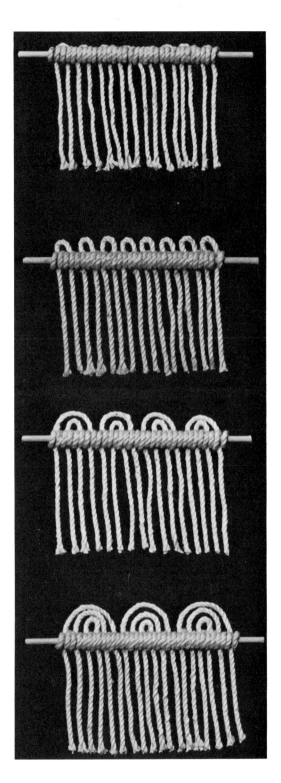

77 *(left)* Double half hitch mounting with small loop. Cord is folded and placed under carrier and pinned. Each end is then hitched to carrier. Position of pin dictates size of loop

78 *(right)* Sampler: double half hitch mountings. From top to bottom: simple double half hitch mounting; double half hitch mounting with single loops; scalloped double half hitch mounting formed by mounting two cords together; scalloped double half hitch mounting formed by mounting three cords together

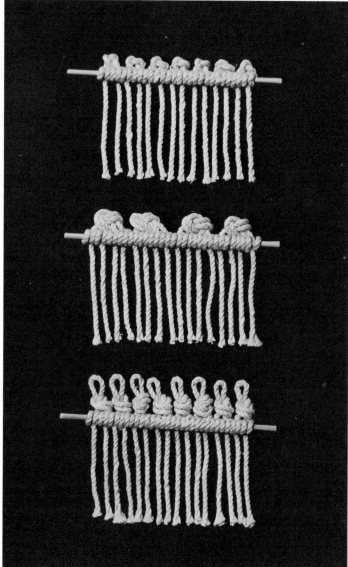

79 *(left)* Overhand knot mounting.
Overhand knot is tied into cord before it
is hitched to carrier

80 *(right)* Sampler: overhand knot
mountings. From top to bottom:
overhand knots tied in single strands; the
same tied in double strands; overhand
knot formed in loop before hitching

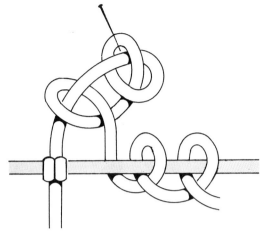

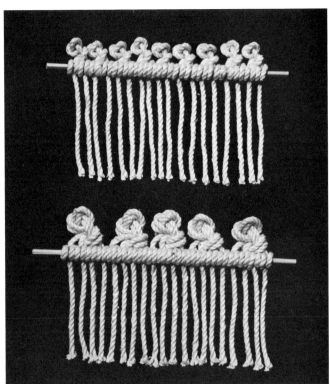

81 *(left)* Chained mounting. Beginning
of half hitch chain is worked before cord
is hitched to carrier

82 *(right)* Sampler: chained mountings.
Above Chain worked in single strand.
Below Chain worked in double strand

83 Flat knot mounting. Flat knot is tied
with two cords (four ends) before the ends
are hitched to carrier. Pins form
decorative loops

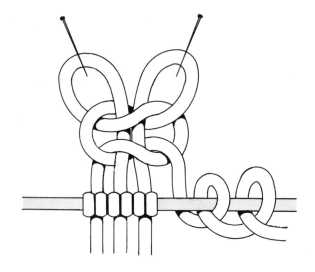

84 Sampler: flat knot mountings. *Above
left* Simple flat knot mounting, knot is
pulled tightly before ends are hitched to
carrier. *Above right* Flat knot mounting
with loops, cords are pinned before tying
flat knot to form decorative loops. *Below
left* Flat knot tied with three folded
cords, the central cord is not actually tied
but acts as carrying cord and forms large
central loop. *Below right* Combination of
flat and overhand knots, mounting tied
with three folded cords, the central cord
forms overhand knot, the outside cords
form flat knot

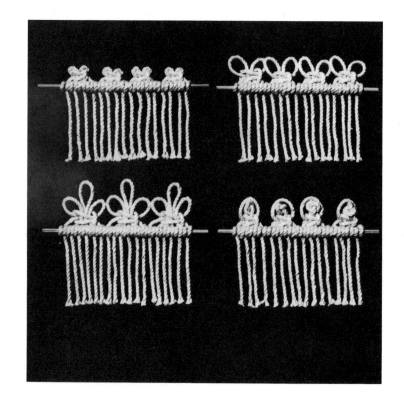

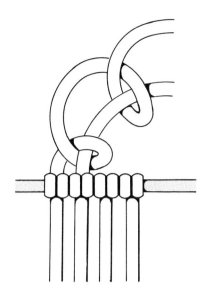

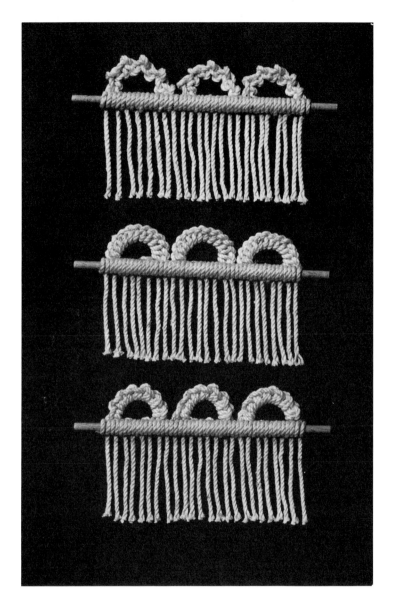

85 *(left)*　Scalloped edge to be formed by hitching one cord over another before mounting. Cords are mounted in centre with simple double half hitch mounting

86 *(right)*　Sampler: scalloped mountings. From top to bottom: scallop formed by chaining; scallop formed by half hitches; scallop formed by reversed double half hitches

The most logical thing to do with the ends left when an article is finished, is to leave them, trim them and perhaps knot a fringe. Open ends often greatly enhance the beauty of a knotted piece and this special aspect of macramé should be utilised wherever possible. The free-hanging ends in the suspended hanging in figure 141 are essential to the grace and balance of the structure.

If the free ends tend to unravel and this is not desirable, make overhand knots, or wax the ends. Overhand knots have been tied in the sampler in figure 72 to prevent the nylon seine twine from unravelling. Various elaborate knots may also serve this purpose. Modified hangman's knots decorate the ends of the knotted structure in figure 143, while the unravelled ends of *Winter Ptarmigan* (figure 74) are effectively combined with figure-eight knots. Unravelled ends such as these are very often effective and this possibility should not be overlooked. The unravelled nylon cords in the dance mask in figure 154 not only contribute to the design but are used by the dancers to great effect.

Macramé ends are also decorated with beads, feathers or other small items. The flower hanging in figure 48 has been given the finishing touch by the generous use of various wooden beads. Chapter 7 has many examples of cord ends being enhanced by the addition of small objects.

The formation of small tassels created by wrapping a coil is yet another possibility. This is demonstrated in figure 55. The detail of the handbag in figure 107 shows the use of such tassels to give a finished look to free ends.

Occasionally it is necessary to eliminate hanging ends altogether. In this case the ends must be taken to the back, or inside and secured there. One method is simply to thread the ends through the knotting to the back with a crochet hook or large-eyed needle, and then hand-stitch the ends down. If the cord is not suitable for sewing, the ends may be glued down. For a more finished edge, a facing is machine-stitched to the ends, folded back over the piece and hand-stitched into place.

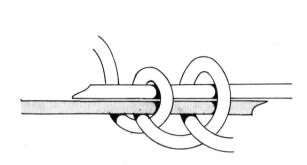

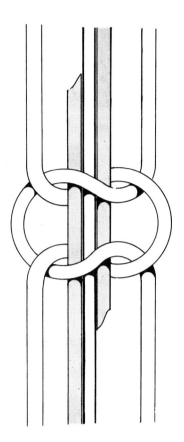

87 *(left)* Method used to replace cord inside row of double half hitching

88 *(right)* Method used to replace cord inside flat knot sennit

REPLACING AND ADDING CORDS

Sometimes, despite the most careful planning, cord runs out in the middle of a piece and must be replaced. Or perhaps the artist wishes to add cords for width or colour.

In free form pieces cords may easily be added and dropped by bringing them into areas of double half hitching. The ends may be either pulled to the back or used as part of the design. In more formal work, cords may be added inside a row of double half hitches (figure 87) or inside a flat knot sennit (figure 88). In both cases the cord being replaced is a carrying cord and hence the ends are hidden inside the knotting cords. A knotting cord may be replaced by tying the end of a new cord to it but in this case the ends must be pulled behind the piece, trimmed, and sewn or glued into place.

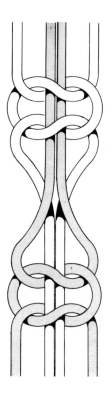

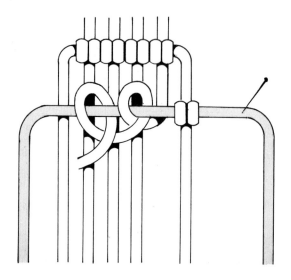

89 *(left)* When working ends of sennit become too short to be knotted they may be switched with the inside cords. Note also that when distance is left between the flat knots, an interesting design appears, which is especially effective when worked in two colours

90 *(right)* Method of adding new cord to sections of double half hitching. New cord is introduced as horizontal carrying cord. The long ends of this cord then become knotting cords as the piece is continued

When the knotting ends of a sennit begin to run out they may be simply exchanged with the longer inside cords (figure 89).

The simplest way to add new width to a piece is to introduce the new cord from the side, by hitching the cords already in the piece over it. The new cord should be long enough for the ends to be employed as knotting cords (figure 90). Figure 48 was increased from six working ends to thirty-eight by this method. Cords may easily be added anywhere in double half hitching by hitching them into place wherever desired. If the cord is introduced with an equally generous amount of cord on both ends, these ends may be then knotted into the piece. If shorter, they may be either pulled behind or left as part of the design.

5 The versatile knot

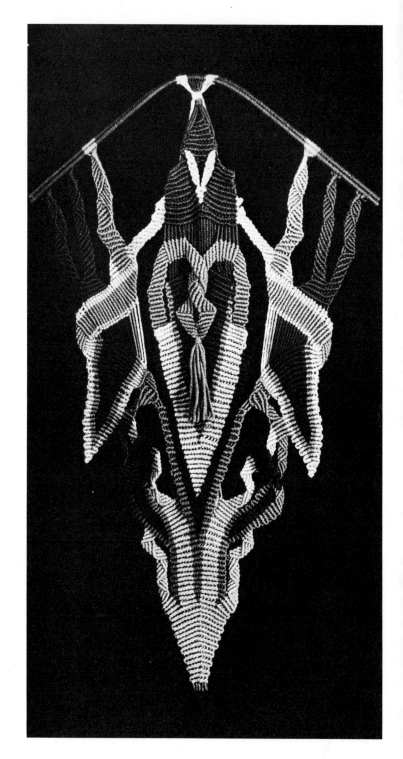

91   Hanging, 135 cm × 75 cm (4 ft 5 in. ×
2 ft 6 in.), Barbara Wittenberg. Knotted
in rug wool in various shades of green.
Colour moves and flows through the
piece by the controlled use of double half
hitches. This hanging was started from
three separate points at the bottom and
worked up. *Collection of Mr and Mrs Harvey
Sibrack*

92 *(opposite)*   Hanging *(detail)*, Barbara
Wittenberg

68

Macramé is an art form evolved from the knotting of fibres. Working from a simple base of two or more knots, macramé artists have created art objects encompassing a remarkable range of form, texture, dimension and colour.

The textural qualities of a piece depend largely on the type of fibre selected: fine or coarse, heavy or delicate, natural or man-made. The type of knot used and the pattern selected also influence the textural quality of the finished piece. Density of patterns or knots creates a heaviness or sturdiness. An example of such dense knotting is the Cavandoli work in figure 14. On the other hand, open knotting evokes a feeling of lightness and airiness. It is well-suited to the delicate bird motif in figure 94. Raised or three-dimensional knots or wrapping will add depth and textural interest to the surface (figure 98).

Often the functional aspect of a piece dictates its size, as in a purse or belt. When macramé is explored as a non-functional art medium, dimension becomes an important aspect of the total expression. Françoise Grossen is primarily occupied with knotting on a very large scale (figure 99) whereas Jean Battles is virtually a miniaturist in macramé. One section of alternating flat knots in the necklace in colour plate 2 is only 4 cm ($1\frac{1}{2}$ in.) wide yet contains twenty-four strands.

Generally speaking, the larger the object, the greater the diameter of the selected cords will be. However, monumental structures have also been created by a careful manipulation and interknotting of relatively fine cords.

Colour in macramé may be handled in two ways; by adding colourful objects such as beads or feathers and/or by the manipulation of coloured fibres. The principle behind colour control is that the cord which is knotted over another will display its colour while at the same time hiding the colour of the carrying cord. Double half hitches, handled carefully, can create flowing lines of colour in a piece (see figure 91). Flat and half knot sennits are also used to carry one colour while covering another. The outside knots hide the colour of the carrying cords inside the sennit.

Elementary as this principle may be, practice is often necessary to gain precise control over the movement of colour in knotting. It is often difficult for the less experienced knotter to visualize at the beginning of the piece just which cords will be knotted and where. In early experiments with different coloured cords, one basic rule may be helpful. If cords are mounted in a symmetrical colour sequence from the centre out and the piece is knotted symmetrically, some sort of regular colour pattern will emerge. The hanging in figure 93 illustrates this principle. A hanging or belt mounted and knotted in this manner serves as a useful learning experience for a beginner. When a haphazard distribution of colour is desired, the colours may be mounted in any order and the knotting follow any design. This, of course, is the most difficult type of knotting in which to control the colour. Cavandoli, another technique of controlling colour solely through knotting, is discussed in chapter 6.

Without the assistance of extra articles, fancy knots or other crafts to decorate and enhance the knotting, the artists presented in this chapter demonstrate their abilities to utilize the potential of the knot to its fullest. The constructions displayed here have been created solely by the knotting, twisting and wrapping of fibres. These constructions give testimony to the skill of the artists and the versatility of the basic knots.

93   *Pink and Green II*, 60 cm × 25 cm (2 ft × 10 in.), Bonny Schmid-Burleson. Green and pink rug wool was mounted symmetrically from the centre out on a wooden dowel. Knotting of horizontal rows of cording, diamonds and sennits moved the colour through the piece creating an interesting colour pattern. *Collection of Maynard and Elizabeth Burleson*

94 *(opposite)*   *Bird*, 50 cm × 35 cm (1 ft 8 in. × 1 ft 2 in.), Doloros Meisterheim. Hanging of yellow linen cord mounted on whittled osage wood. Pictorial image was formed by careful arrangement of rows of double half hitches

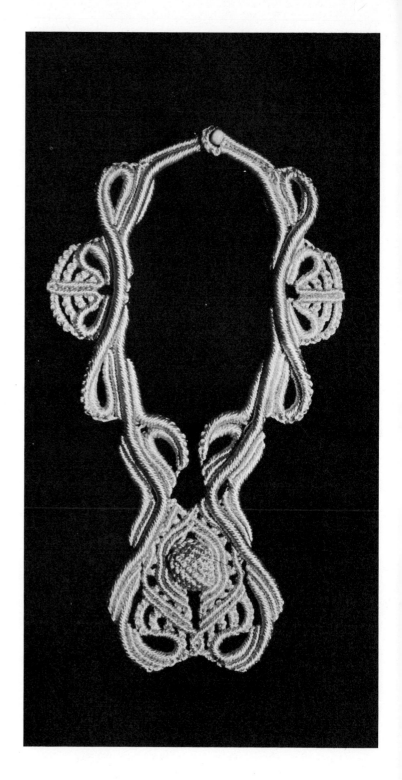

95   Soft jewelry, 35 cm × 20 cm (1 ft
2 in. × 8 in.), Joan Michaels Paque. White
nylon cord knotted into graceful
neckpiece. *Photo Henry Paque*

96 *(opposite)   Configurations,* 30 cm (1 ft)
diameter, Joan Michaels Paque. White
nylon cord worked in double half hitches.
The graphic work of M. C. Escher
influenced the artist to explore the
problem of penetrating planes and their
significance for macramé

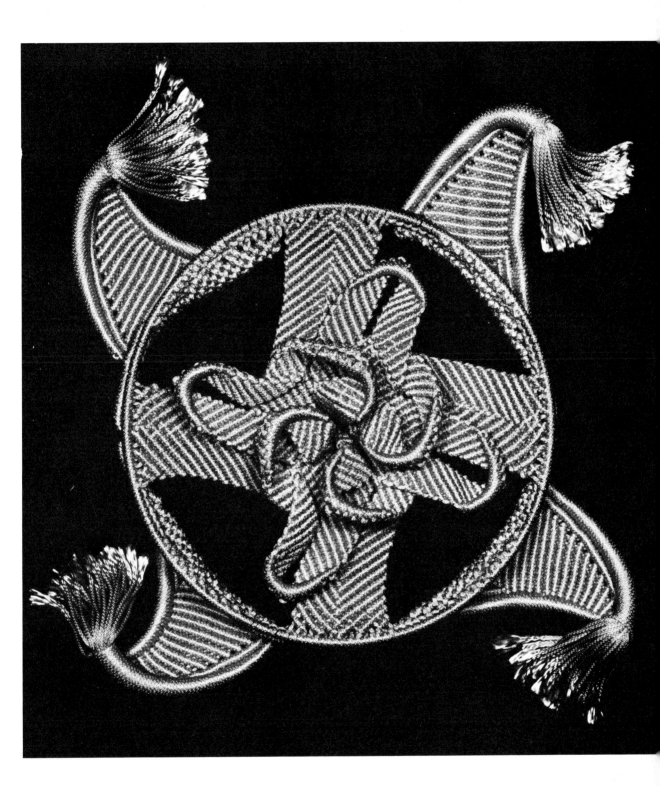

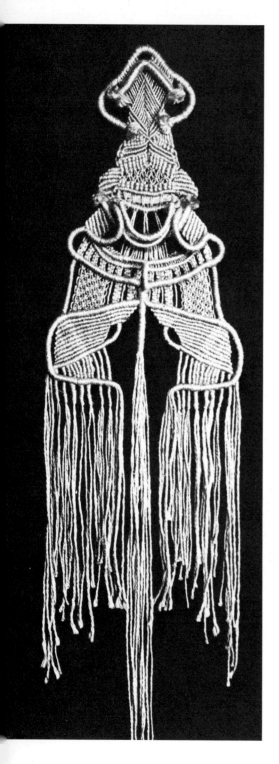

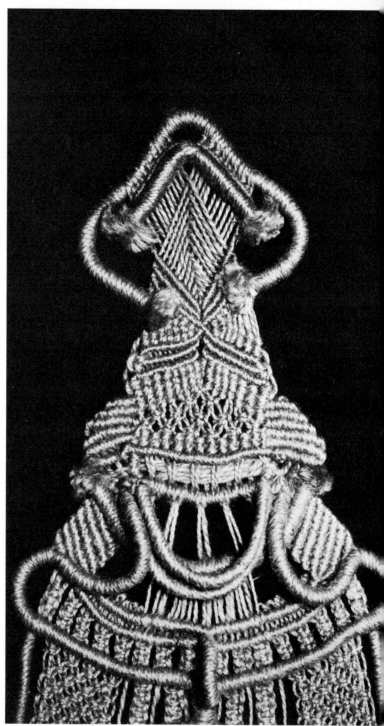

74

97 *(opposite left)* *Separate identities,*
155 cm × 50 cm (5 ft 1 in. × 1 ft 8 in.),
Dorris Akers. Natural and rose dyed jute
arranged in combinations of double half
hitches, flat knots and wrapping

98 *(opposite right)* *Separate identities*
(detail), Dorris Akers. Textural interest
and depth have been added by effective
use of wrapping

99 *Five white elements,* 3·10 m × 1·85 m
(10 ft × 6 ft), Françoise Grossen. This
monumental fibre construction was
knotted in white piping cord. *Photo Tom*
Crane

100 *(overleaf left)* *Ritualis Number 1,*
200 cm × 40 cm (6 ft 7 in. × 1 ft 4 in.),
John Wahling, 5-ply rug linen and natural
jute have been beautifully combined in
this suspended hanging. Piece was
developed through the use of double half
hitches, overhand knots and braiding

101 *(overleaf right)* *Ritualis Number 1*
(detail), Jon Wahling

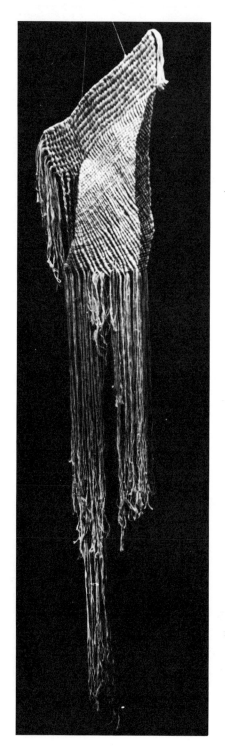

6 Cavandoli

Cavandoli work is a method of working vertical and horizontal double half hitches in contrasting colours. The knotting cord, which is tied over the carrying cord, is the one which will be visible and will hide the other. Hence, if the cords are two different colours, an interplay of colour can be achieved by alternately arranging horizontal and vertical double half hitches (figure 103). With Cavandoli it is thus possible to do figurative or abstract designing, using one colour as the background and another colour for the pattern. The resultant fabric is very firm and closely knotted and may, at first glance, appear to be woven. However, Cavandoli, a non-loom technique, is unlike weaving in that the weft and warp continually exchange functions. In fact, part of the fascination of the technique is that the different areas of colour do have different structural qualities, as the knots are tied in alternate directions. Since it is not limited to a loom or frame as are similar weaving techniques such as Swedish knotting, Cavandoli work may take any shape the artist desires, be it free-form or geometric.

The densely knotted Cavandoli fabric is sturdy and well suited to the construction of handbags or wall tapestries. Cavandoli may be a trim or introduction to a larger knotted piece as in figure 107, or the body of a piece with macramé trim as in figure 109.

The technique is in principle very simple, if somewhat time consuming. It lends itself extremely well to work where the artist prefers to have the piece completely designed before the knotting is begun. It is usually planned beforehand on graph paper, each square representing a knot. If the vertical cords are light, the darkened spaces would represent the areas where the darker horizontal cord is to be knotted over the lighter vertical ones (figure 104).

102 Sampler, Joan Michaels Paque. Small Cavandoli sampler in beige and brown twine. Light cords form vertical double half hitches, the darker cords the horizontal ones

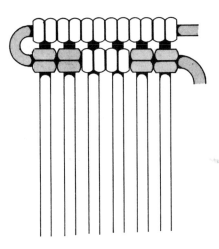

103 Cavandoli technique. When dark cord is knotted over light cord, dark knots are visible and *vice versa*

78

1 2 3 4 5 6 7 8 9 10 11 12 13 14 15 16 17 18 19 20 21 22 23 24 25 26 27 28 29 30 31 32

104 Cavandoli butterfly design on graph paper. ×'s represent areas where yellow horizontal cord will be hitched over green vertical cords to form yellow outline of a butterfly

105 Green and yellow shoulder bag, Bonny Schmid-Burleson. Green rug wool was mounted on circular mounting cord. Yellow rug wool was used as horizontal cord to form butterfly pattern in vertical double half hitches. Bag was knotted in one piece in a circular manner and knotted together across bottom. Braided shoulder strap sewn to finish it

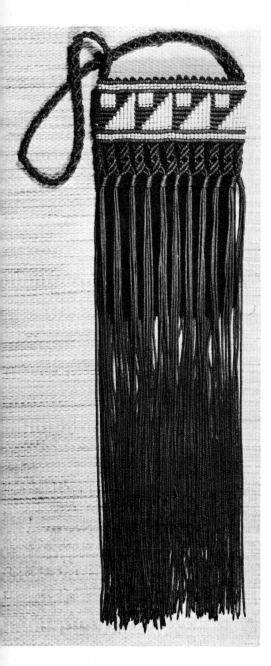

107   Bag *(detail)*, Bonny Schmid-
Burleson. The Cavandoli band is a
knotted interpretation of an American
Plains Indian design, *The Exit Way of Life*.
The macramé repeats the strong diagonals
of the Cavandoli

106   Bag, Bonny Schmid-Burleson.
Burgundy suède leather trimmed with
band of Cavandoli and macramé in
natural and burgundy dyed polished hemp

When designing Cavandoli work it should be noted that
figurative designs will be of a geometric nature. Also, if the
pattern is composed of the vertical double half hitches, it will be
somewhat elongated as the vertical hitches are taller than the
horizontal ones. This should be kept in mind when the design is
being planned on graph paper. It may be necessary to plan the
pattern shorter than the desired result to allow for this elongation.

To begin with, the cords are mounted and hung vertically,
usually in one colour. One very long cord in a contrasting colour
is brought back and forth across the hanging cords, sometimes
as a carrying cord, sometimes as a knotting cord, depending on
the pattern.

108 Jug with pre-Colombian motif,
50 cm (1 ft 8 in.) high, Gervaise
Livingstone. Natural linen and black
mohair knotted to cover jug. *Photo
Morton Witz*

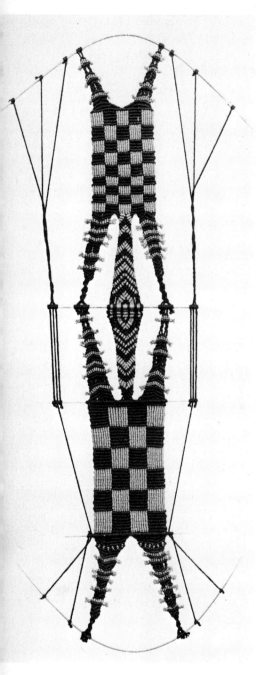

As Cavandoli work is very dense, the vertical cords should be measured at least seven times the desired finished length. The horizontal cord may be calculated by generously estimating the number of times the cord will cross the piece and multiplying this by the width of the piece. This would be the length needed to go back and forth *without knotting*. As the cord will also be knotted, this length is multiplied by seven. This long cord should be rolled into a bundle and held with a rubber band. If the piece is to be very large, this bundle can become unmanageable. In this case, shorter lengths are used, new cords being added when the need arises, (see figure 15 for an example of cord measurement for macramé and Cavandoli).

Cavandoli need not be limited to two colours. Additional colour can be easily added to a row of double half hitches by exchanging the horizontal cord for a new coloured cord. The vertical colours may also be exchanged by dropping these cords off and tying the ends of the cords to different coloured cords. The exchange of colour in the hanging, figure 14, has been achieved in this manner. Naturally, more colour may be introduced by mounting two or more colours as the vertical cords.

The art of the American Indian is a rich source of inspiration for Cavandoli work. Especially in bead work and basketry one can find an apparently infinite array of intriguing and handsome geometric designs. For instance, the Cavandoli knotting in figure 106 was inspired by a motif employed by the American Plains Indians.

The Cavandoli technique can appear deceptively simple and as such limited. However, the artist willing to recognize the potential of this extremely controlled technique will find that it offers great freedom in figurative and abstract designing and unlimited possibilities of colour exchanges within a space. It needs only the creative knotter to make it come alive.

109   *Spirit of Do,* 200 cm × 60 cm
(6 ft 7 in. × 2 ft), Bonny Schmid-Burleson.
Large wall hanging in red and black rug
wool. Design inspired by dance mask of
the African Bobo tribe

82

7 Macramé pot-pourri

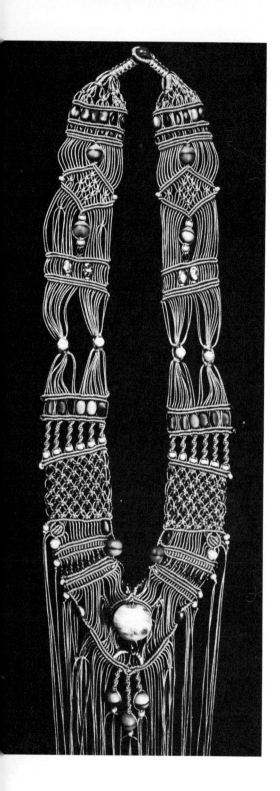

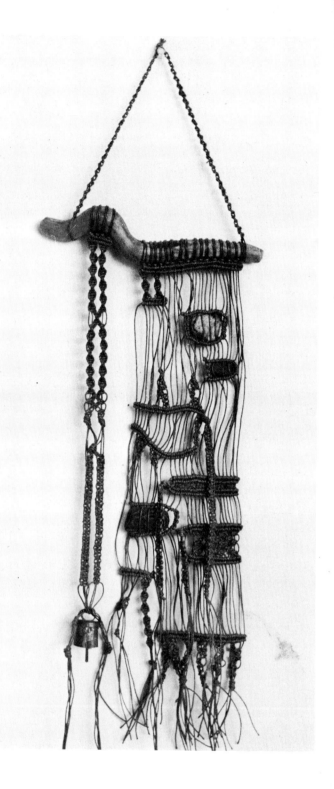

The only essential material for macramé is the knottable cord. However, to add a new dimension, many artists have chosen to include various items and materials other than cords. Additional objects may add colour, texture and depth as well as enhance the total design. Beads, feathers, driftwood, bells and rocks are just some of the articles which have been successfully incorporated into macramé work.

Any items selected for macramé should be studied with regard to textural quality, size, shape and colour in relation to the respective qualities of the fibres to be used and the design intended for the entire piece. There are no hard and fast rules as skilful artists have managed to combine almost every imaginable type of object within a vast array of varied designs. It is, however, especially important that any articles worked into knotted pieces be an integral part of the total artistic concept. Articles may be added when a knotted piece is finished. Items such as feathers or beads can often be effectively introduced to a completed piece if they support the unity of the design. Frequent experimentation and the willingness to try many different approaches will give the knotter the experience needed to be able to decide what belongs in a composition and what does not.

The object most frequently combined with macramé is perhaps the bead. This item comes in a variety of sizes, shapes, colours and textures. Beads can often give the right decorative accent to accessories such as belts and jewelry. They are also used to decorate the ends of a wall hanging and may, of course, be incorporated into the body of a hanging itself. Other small objects such as buttons, shells, or feathers may also be used.

If the hole of a bead is too small it may be difficult or impossible to string. In this case enlarge the hole with a pair of small scissors. Moreover, stringing may be facilitated by trimming the ends of cords to a sharp point and dipping them in wax. Holes for threading may also be drilled into some small items, such as buttons or shells.

110 *(opposite left)* Necklace, Jean Battles. The delicate knotting of light steel blue upholstery twine is accentuated by a variety of beads in reds, oranges, blues, purples and dark greys

111 *(opposite right)* Driftwood hanging, 60 cm × 25 cm (24 in. × 10 in.), Marilyn Blair. Small brown hanging of granite flax twine was mounted on driftwood. Small pieces of driftwood and an Indian bell have been incorporated into the piece. *Photo Thomas D. Cohen*

112 *The sea*, 180 cm × 90 cm (5 ft 11 in. × 3 ft), Barbara Wittenberg. Large knotted portrait of the sea in natural jute and rayon with driftwood mounting. The net symbolizes waves, and the whirlpools of the tide are formed by a circle. The jute captures the texture and colour of the sand while the white and pale green rayon delicately suggests sea foam. Rocks and small glass beads have been subtly worked into the piece as the natural representatives of the things of the sea

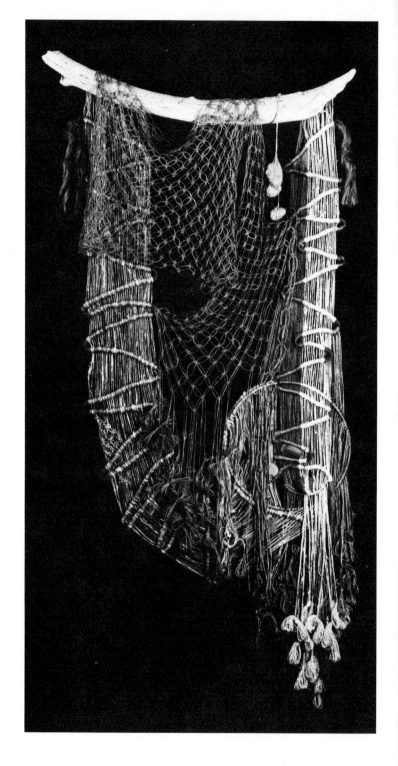

113 *(opposite)   The sea (detail)*, Barbara Wittenberg. Stones collect inside the knotted whirlpool of the tide

Small objects may also be woven or wrapped into the work. Lighter pieces such as feathers are held in place attractively by wrapping as in figure 126. Heavier items such as wood or stones must be secured by knotting or weaving (figure 111). Ingenious methods have been devised by artists for fastening items onto a piece. Barbara Wittenberg crocheted small nets to hold the stones she worked into her large driftwood hanging in figure 112.

An observant collector who is able to explore a wood should easily gather a good supply of bark, sticks, pine cones, grasses and so forth which can then be worked into the appropriate macramé pieces. Beach wanderers likewise can amass delightful collections of shells, feathers, driftwood and stones. Larger driftwood pieces make excellent beginnings for wall hangings as in figures 111 and 112. Materials found in nature show great diversity in texture, form and colour which the creative knotter can use to enhance and supplement the knotted fibres.

Objects introduced into macramé need not, of course, be only natural. Man-made items, if carefully selected, are also of great interest. Antique shops provide a wealth of supplies such as old beads, jewelry pieces, copper, glass or coins. With skill and imagination all this can be beautifully worked into macramé. An afternoon spent in a junk shop may offer as its reward a collection of intriguing pieces of old metal, old chair legs, harness parts and the like. An interesting aspect of the hanging illustrated in figure 115 is the contrast between the natural jute and the metal sections of an old stove.

Some artists prefer to design and make supplementary objects themselves. The ceramics artist can design beads, abstract forms or jewelry pieces and then incorporate them into macramé work. A ceramic sculpture may be designed for the explicit purpose of being combined with knotted fibres. Marianne Rodwell's work in figure 1 is an outstanding example of this type of craftsmanship.

114   *Red mountain*, 45 cm × 25 cm
(18 in. × 10 in.), Virginia Davis. Small tan
and brown hanging of waxed twine and
marlin cord, effectively combined with
cowry shells, Indian bone beads, blue
glass and pheasant feathers. *Photo Martin
Davis*

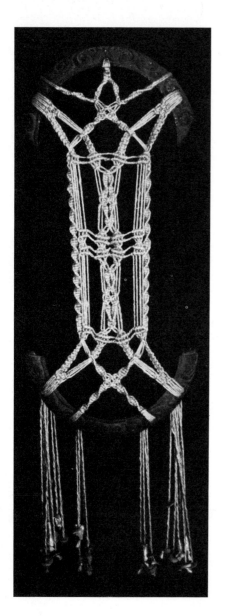

By the supplemental use of various objects the artist often creates a work which, aside from its aesthetic appeal, is also a personal statement. The artist naturally selects articles of personal value and interest. It has been seen that very often those who have incorporated various items into a knotted piece show strong personal attachments to that particular work. The piece might suggest a closeness to something of nature – a bird, the sea, a beach, (figure 112). It might reveal memories of childhood, (figure 118). Such an arrangement of knotted fibres and objects has a great nostalgic and subjective quality for viewer and creator alike.

115   Hanging, 120 cm × 40 cm (4 ft × 1 ft 4 in.), Terri Buchen. Natural jute knotted between two pieces of metal from an old stove. Handmade ceramic beads decorate ends of cord. *Collection of Dorris Akers*

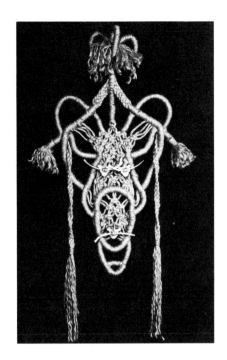

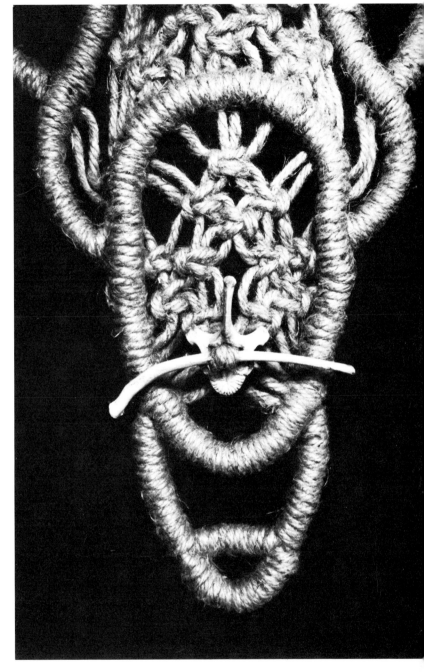

116 *(left)* *Walloon*, 140 cm × 80 cm (4 ft
7 in. × 2 ft 7 in.), Dorris Akers. 5-ply
natural jute tube rope has been wrapped,
knotted and braided into a large open
hanging. Bones are calf's ribs and
vertebrae
117 *(right)* *Walloon (detail)*, Dorris
Akers

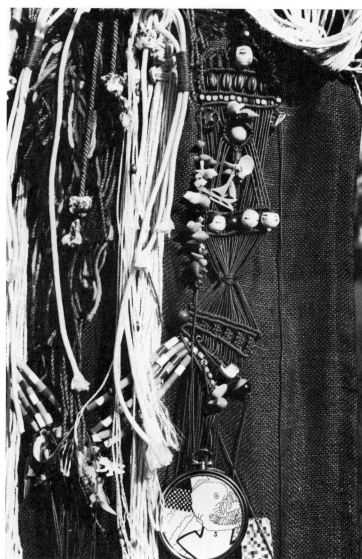

92

118 *(opposite left)* Macramé on cloth, 85 cm × 60 cm (2 ft 9 in. × 1 ft 11 in.), Jean Battles. Personal statement reminiscent of childhood and children. Beads, toys, photographs and drawings are arranged within a variety of cords

119 *(opposite right)* Macramé on cloth *(detail)*, Jean Battles. Small colourful toys are easily visible

120 *Primitif (detail)*, Marianne S. Rodwell. *(See figure 1)*

121 *Assemblage,* 80 cm × 50 cm (2 ft
7 in. × 1 ft 8 in.), Dorris Akers. Wood,
ropes, bone, fungi, metal pieces and
feathers combined by knotting and
wrapping cords

94

8 Mixed media

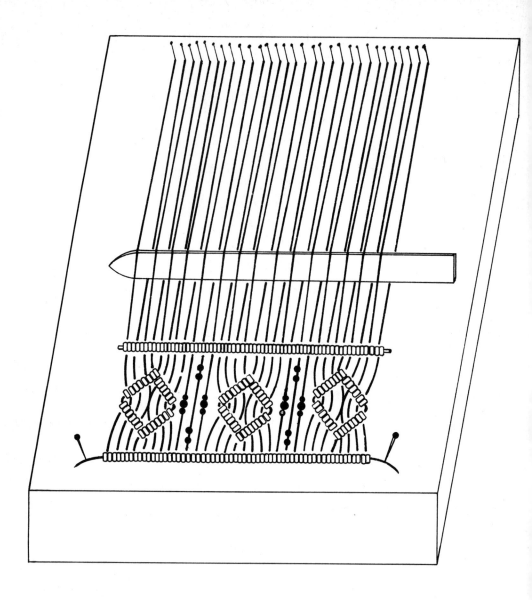

122 Temporary loom on knotting board for combining weaving with macramé. Macramé piece is pinned upside down on board with each vertical cord fastened separately and firmly to form warp. Shed sword is inserted to build first shed. Second shed must be opened with the fingers, or, if the area to be woven is large, string heddles may be attached

Plate 3 *Double wings*, 190 cm × 130 cm (6 ft 3 in. × 4 ft 3 in.), Jon Wahling. Free-standing structure of dyed jute knotted in double half hitches

96

One of the most fascinating new developments of contemporary crafts is the challenge presented by mixed media. Many artists working in crafts today do not limit themselves to the exploration of one craft in a single project. Rather, they are expanding their range of artistic means through the innovative combination of various crafts. Indeed, a large number of people who have contributed their work to this book are not primarily involved in knotting. The work shown here was done by people from such diverse artistic professions as weaving, spinning, ceramics, sculpture, painting, glass blowing, leather and metal work. They are all enthusiastic about the possibilities offered by knotting as a complement to and extension of their particular craft.

As the practice of mixing many of these crafts is new, artists must often devise new techniques for combinations when the need arises. Experimentation and inventiveness are necessary as is a thorough understanding of the crafts involved. Care must be taken that the total unity of a piece is strengthened by the combination of media, not weakened.

Macramé, itself a textile art, may often be combined with other textile crafts to very great advantage. The combination of knotting with weaving is not new. Knotting the warp ends to form a fringe to a woven garment is an ancient practice. Here, knotting served a supplementary decorative function. Today, knotting is no longer restricted to its former purpose of fringing but is being used dynamically in combination with weaving. Artists are integrating small areas of weaving into knotted structures to add textural interest. Knotting and weaving are also being combined as partners, each playing an equally important role in the construction of a piece.

123 *Joseph's coat*, 130 cm × 115 cm
(4 ft 3 in. × 3 ft 9 in.), Clara Creager.
Woven areas arranged with sennits and
alternating flat knots. Hanging mounted
on found iron frame. Wool is ochre,
brown, grey and white. *Photo Charles
Vorhees*

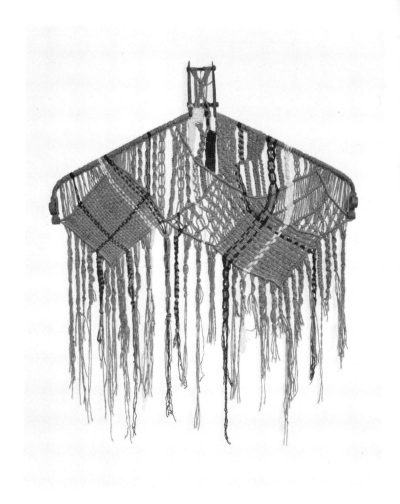

Weaving is perhaps the craft most commonly combined with
macramé. It can decorate the inside of a diamond or the space
between rows of double half hitching (figure 123). In fact exami-
nation of many of the illustrations throughout this book will
also reveal such areas decorated with weaving, as in figure 150.
If the area is small the weaving may be done with the fingers or
with a crochet hook. For larger areas the knotter may wish to
devise a temporary loom to be used while the weaving is in
progress. One method of doing this on the knotting board is
shown in figure 122. It is also possible to weight the ends of the
vertical cords to form a more stationary warp.

124 Untitled, 60 cm × 50 cm
(24 in. × 20 in.), Mary Waldhart. Woven
and knotted construction of handspun
goat hair in natural black and white.
Weaving frame has been retained, creating
an effective setting for the fibres. *Photo
Neil Waldhart*

125 Untitled *(detail)*, Mary Waldhart.
Centre section consists of flat knots and
vertical double half hitches knotted over
warp thread. *Photo Neil Waldhart*

While weaving and knotting are extremely compatible, weaving is not the only textile craft to be combined with knotting. Textile artists have designed and executed unusual pieces combining knotting with rug hooking, crochet, knitting and sewing (figures 59 and 132). Knotters frequently dye their own fibres (an art in itself) and cords or finished pieces may be tye-dyed. A number of knotters spin some of their own fibres to acquire the right natural texture (figure 129). Knotting in combination with leather work is often an effective method of giving a leather article a decorative accent, as in the suède and hemp purse in figure 106.

126   *Africanus no 1,* 130 cm × 35 cm
(4 ft 3 in. × 1 ft 2 in.), Barbara Wittenberg.
Combination of Swedish knotting, which
is actually a weaving technique with
macramé. Centre, in shades of orange,
was worked separately on a frame in
Swedish knotting. Tail and upper part
worked in double half hitches and
attached. Feathers add primitive emphasis.
Collection of Dr and Mrs Gerald Aptekar

127 *(opposite)   Africanus no 1 (detail),*
Barbara Wittenberg

128 *Sun medallion,* 155 cm (5 ft) diameter, Marianne S. Rodwell. Vitality and energy characterize this colourful wall piece of knotted, wrapped and woven fibres. Jute, hemp and rug wool are worked over a wooden frame. Centre of medallion is a mirror. Wooden and bamboo beads are interspersed throughout. *Photographed at Cardinal Stritch College, Milwaukee, Wisconsin, USA*

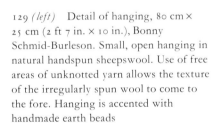

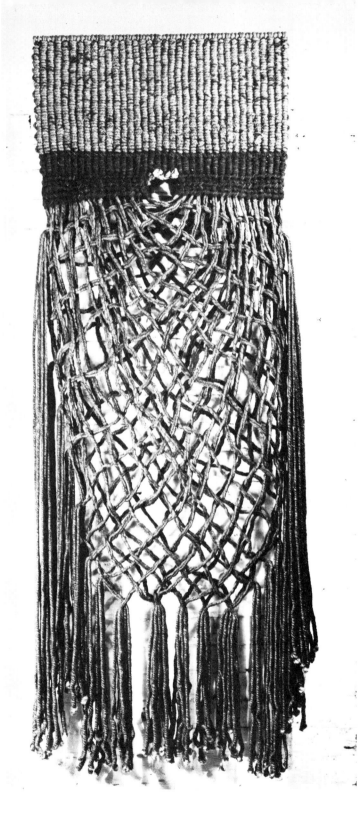

129 *(left)* Detail of hanging, 80 cm ×
25 cm (2 ft 7 in. × 10 in.), Bonny
Schmid-Burleson. Small, open hanging in
natural handspun sheepswool. Use of free
areas of unknotted yarn allows the texture
of the irregularly spun wool to come to
the fore. Hanging is accented with
handmade earth beads

130 *(right)* *Space,* 180 cm × 65 cm
(6 ft × 2 ft), Jon Wahling. Green jute and
light purple rug wool combine to form
top area of double half hitches from
which large open net-like structure is
suspended. Net is worked in technique
known as Osage braiding where cords
are woven from centre to outside. Wire
has been plyed onto wool in net to
strengthen the fibres

131   *Shield with yak and feathers,*
290 cm × 180 cm (9 ft 6 in. × 6 ft), Gervaise
Livingstone. Monumental shield of woven,
knotted and wrapped handspun Peruvian
and jute yarns, yak and horse hair. Strips
were woven on four harness floor loom
and then rewoven into piece. Feathers and
yak hair secured by half hitches and white
fringe is knotted into place. *Collection of
Shirley Johnston. Photo Morton Witz*

132 Hooked hanging, 130 cm × 35 cm (4 ft 3 in. × 1 ft 2 in.), Evelyn Söllner-Reid. Base of hanging hooked in orange, yellow and brown knitting wools. Double half hitches form rings which protrude from hooked area. Jute ends have also been wrapped in wool, knotted and unravelled to form decorative endings

133 *(right)* Mixed media hanging *(detail)*, Evelyn Söllner-Reid. Cascade of white wool roving contrasts strikingly with the precision of the large wrapped flat knot. See colour plate 1

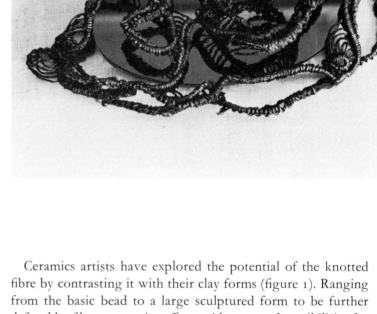

134 *(left)* Lamp, 40 cm (1 ft 4 in.) high, Marianne S. Rodwell. Wheel thrown stoneware lamp suspended and decorated by knotted hemp. *Photographed at Cardinal Stritch College, Milwaukee, Wisconsin, USA*

135 *(right)* Bronze cast hand mirror, 25 cm × 15 cm (10 in. × 6 in.), Kathleen A. Doyle. Hand mirror designed to examine feasibility of combining cast macramé units in a piece of metal work. Twenty-one pieces of bronze were cast separately from linen models and then soldered into the dome shape. Incorporated within the design were finger grips as well as a handle for the viewer to use in holding this piece of jewelry. *Photo Beth Morgan*

Ceramics artists have explored the potential of the knotted fibre by contrasting it with their clay forms (figure 1). Ranging from the basic bead to a large sculptured form to be further defined by fibres, ceramics offer a wide range of possibilities for combination with fibres. The juxtaposition of the two is especially interesting as this emphasizes their contrasting textural qualities. Ceramics offer form, shape and a smoother surface while the fibres provide texture and warmth.

Metal macramé is, at this point, at an experimental stage. Kathleen Doyle, having previously worked in metal, wished to capture the structure of knots in metal. Hence, she has developed the 'Doyle modified casting procedure' to cast metal from a fibre model. This is burned out, during the process leaving units of cast bronze knots. Using this method she is able to create constructions literally of metal knots (figure 135). This innovative procedure should mark the beginning of an entirely new crafts field.

Contemporary crafts are marked by a heightened awareness of and involvement with materials. Using a combination of media to arrange and explore these materials is the natural result of such awareness. Mixed-media is one of the most exciting aspects of crafts today and especially of macramé.

9 The knotted structure

136 *(opposite)* *Double wings (detail)*, Jon Wahling. To achieve textural interest and dimensional variation contrasting areas have been knotted by reversing the double half hitch. See colour plate 3

137 Untitled, 190 cm × 130 cm (6 ft 3 in. × 4 ft 3 in.), Hiromi Oda. Wall piece of knotted and wrapped jute. Feathers and unravelled ends add to organic feel of piece. *Photo Tenjun Kamoshita*

The knot, in itself a small and simple thing, may be used as the basic element for building a complex structure. Employed much as the brick in the construction of a house, it is the unit used by the artist to manipulate fibres so as to create large imposing constructions to be placed on the floor, hung on the wall or suspended. These structures may be entirely self-supporting, as are the hollow knotted spirals in *Levels of Consciousness* by Joan Michaels Paque (figure 140), or receive additional support through metal frames or other armature as in figure 138.

Although the macramé knot is the basic element, the result can hardly be termed macramé, but rather knotted structures. As a free form in space, suspended or self-supporting, these structures have little in common with the traditional flat macramé wall decorations, not to speak of the more functional aspect of macramé as in handbags or belts.

138 *(left)* *Mrs Truby's Garden*, 190 cm ×
35 cm (6 ft 3 in. × 1 ft 2 in.), Ron Franks.
Standing structure of dyed jute mounted
on iron frame. Double half hitches form
interrelated planes

139 *(right)* *Mrs Truby's Garden (detail)*,
Ron Franks. View of planes of double
half hitches

140 *Levels of consciousness*, 46 cm (18 in.)
high × 46 cm (18 in.) wide × 310 cm (10 ft)
long. Joan Michaels Paque. Floor piece
of dyed sisal. Yellow and orange hollow
knotted spirals emerge from blue base.
Spirals of double half hitches are
completely self supporting without the
aid of an armature. Forms are flexible and
may be arranged in various compositions
by artist or viewer, making this a structure
for audience participation. *Photo Henry
Paque*

Fibre work gains a new dimension by entering the world of
non-functional art never before explored by knotters. The
existence of such structures created with purely aesthetic ends
in mind renders the debate over the artistic importance of crafts
meaningless. Textile work, always respected as age-old crafts,
is now taking its rightful place along side the traditional media
in contemporary museums, in galleries and in the homes of
private collectors.

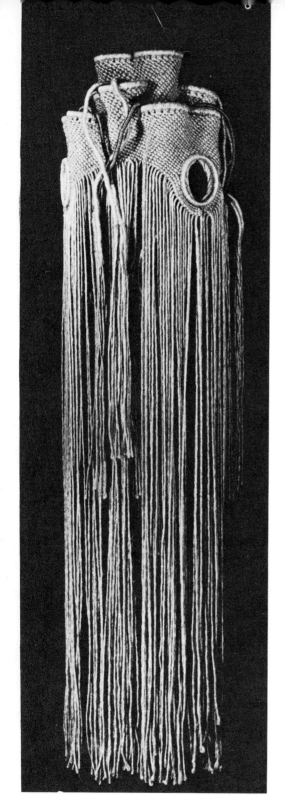

141 *(left)* Hanging sculpture, 180 cm
(5 ft 11 in.), Esther Parada. Wrapped and
knotted natural jute forms shapes inside
and outside hanging. Piece includes very
small amount of delicate brown and green
wrapping. *Photographed at the American
Craftsman, Chicago, Illinois, USA*

142 *(right)* Hanging sculpture *(detail)*,
Esther Parada

Structural knotting, in departing from the flat traditional macramé, allows the artist to explore the relationship between three-dimensional form and space. Space is as integral to the design as the form itself. This is especially evident in the suspended hanging in figure 142 in which the movement of the cords inside the hollow structure is as important as that outside. The knot itself is three-dimensional but only when tied on a very large scale does this characteristic become evident as more space is controlled. The lanyard knot in *Consciousness III* (figure 146) becomes a structural design element on its own by virtue of its size. *Contact* (figure 145) is particularly interesting as relatively few knots incorporate a large amount of space making this an imposing construction.

Warmth, texture and tactility are qualities inherent in fibres. This work offers the artist the possibility of exploring these qualities along with the traditional ones of form, colour and design. Unlike those who look at paintings, the viewer of fibre art is drawn to explore the work through the sense of touch. Indeed, to appreciate fully the sensitive choice of materials in Ritualis I (figure 100), one should handle the jute and the linen and actually feel the contrast between the soft fringe and the firm knots.

The art of knotting lends itself particularly well to the exploration of various textures, combinations of different fibres and techniques. The knotted constructions illustrated in this chapter are a contemporary expression of artists using knotting as an art form based upon superb craftsmanship.

143   *Personage,* 150 cm × 70 cm (4 ft 11 in. × 2 ft 3 in.), Aurelia Munoz. Red and copper coloured sisal knotted in double half hitches to form body. Monkey's fists and modified hangman's knots worked into ends. *Photo Ramon Calvet Studio*

Plate 4   *Mask with feathers (detail)*, Bonny Schmid-Burleson. Colour selection was influenced by study of masks and figures of Northwest American Indians

144 *Albino black knotting* 250 cm
(8 ft 6 in.) high, Gervaise Livingstone.
Monumental structure knotted with
3·5 cm (1¼ in.) white welting cord.
Reversed double half hitches used to
mount cords onto wire frame. *Photo
Morton Witz*

145 *(opposite)   Contact (detail)*, 310 cm ×
680 cm (10 ft × 22 ft), Françoise Grossen.
Knotted construction consisting of a total
of seven elements in white cotton piping
cord. *Photo Tom Crane*

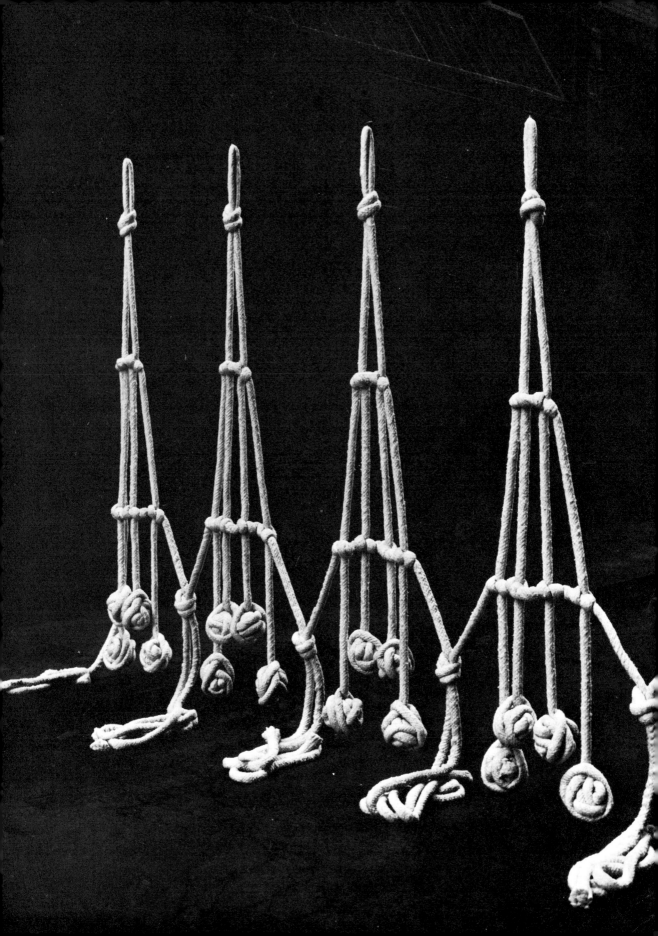

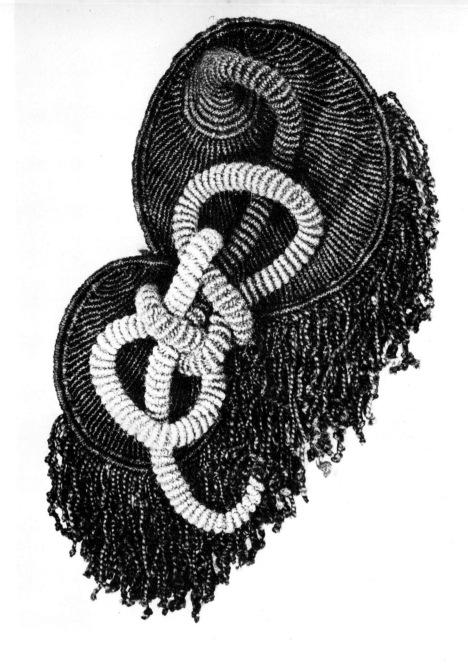

146 *Consciousness III,* 140 cm × 35 cm
(4 ft 7 in. × 1 ft 2 in.), Joan Michaels
Paque. Base of knotted blue and purple
dyed sisal. Extension is hollow tube of
dyed sisal which gradually changes from
dark to light orange. Entire coil is
knotted before it is tied into large
lanyard knot and tacked to base

147 *(opposite)   Consciousness III (detail),*
Joan Michaels Paque

116

148 Untitled, 120 cm × 90 cm (3 ft 11 in.
× 2 ft 11 in.), Claire Zeisler. Base of wall
piece constructed of alternating flat knots
in red wool. Wool forms shallow bowl in
which short sections of natural bast are
held

10 Variations on a theme: a gallery of masks

One of the most dramatic and powerful forms of art is the mask. As a cultural mirror to mankind it has long been an intriguing and compelling subject for artists. The mask, as an abstraction of the human face that can often be reduced to basic geometric elements, is a subject especially suited to macramé.

The first step from, say, a wooden African mask to a knotted mask has been made by African craftsmen themselves, who used knotted fibres to support or decorate a mask. Macramé artists, carrying this step further, are now making masks entirely of knotted and twisted fibres. From a literal interpretation of a specific primitive mask to a freely developed variation or fantasy, the construction of a fibre mask reflects the age-old fascination with the human face and its emotions. This chapter presents a gallery of masks by macramé artists as they continue a powerful tradition.

149   Mask with feathers, 80 cm (2 ft 7 in.) long, Bonny Schmid-Burleson. Wool, hemp and cotton cords knotted and woven into mask. Sandalwood beads, pods and feathers add dramatic accent

150 *Saibai mask,* 80 cm (2 ft 7 in.) long,
Bonny Schmid-Burleson. Knotted mask
inspired by wood and fibre mask from
the Island of Saibai. Jute, sisal, hemp,
wool and cotton cords in orange, white
and browns have been knotted in double
half hitches and alternating flat knots to
form mask. Cords were mounted on
metal frame along crown but dimensional
shape of mask is held by the strength of
the knots alone

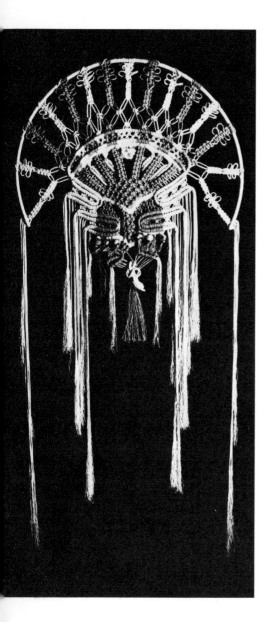

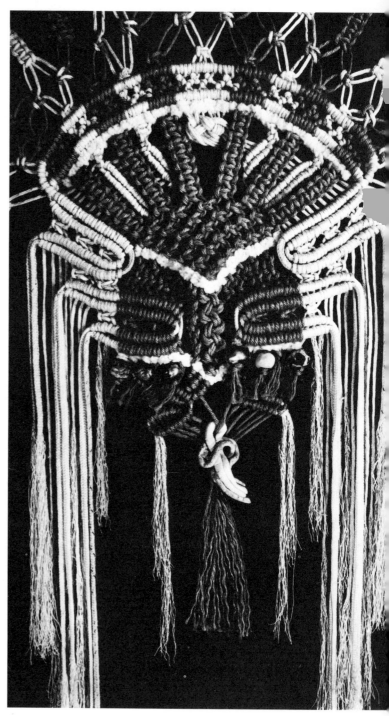

151 *(left)* Mask, 140 cm × 70 cm (4 ft
7 in. × 2 ft 3 in.), Barbara Wittenberg.
Nylon and jute in browns and white in
controlled arrangement of double half
hitches, sennits and alternating flat knots

152 *(right)* Mask *(detail)*, Barbara
Wittenberg

122

153 Mask, 120 cm (3 ft 11 in.) long, Ron
Franks. Dramatic mask intended as floor
piece. Silvery life cast of artist's face
contrasts strikingly with black feathers.
Knotting plays invisible supporting role
as entire back of mask is composed of flat
knotted jute, the ends of which emerge
along the face. This knotting is used to
hold feathers in place and to support the
mask on the floor. Feathers on end of jute
are held by wrapped wire. *Courtesy of Ohio
Dominican College, Columbus, Ohio, USA*

154 Dance mask, Jimmie L. Benedict. One of a pair of masks made for choreographic production. Mask is constructed of various sizes of dyed twisted nylon cord. This mask is in greens and blues to represent cool side of person's identity. Companion mask is identical but in yellow and purples for the warm side. Mask laces up back to conform to wearer's head. *Photo William R. Benedict*

155 *(opposite left)* Mask, 45 cm (1 ft 6 in.), Bonny Schmid-Burleson. Small yellow and black oriental mask of wool and hemp. Beads decorate face and are used to form teeth. *Collection of Mr and Mrs Robert Criddle*

156 *(opposite right)* Mask, 90 cm × 40 cm (2 ft 11 in. × 1 ft 4 in.), Imelda Manalo-Pesch. Abstract knotted mask of natural sisal and black, green, orange and yellow rug wool. *Photo Hy Rosen*

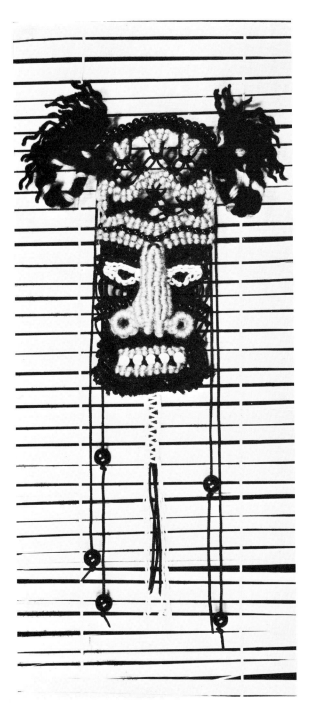

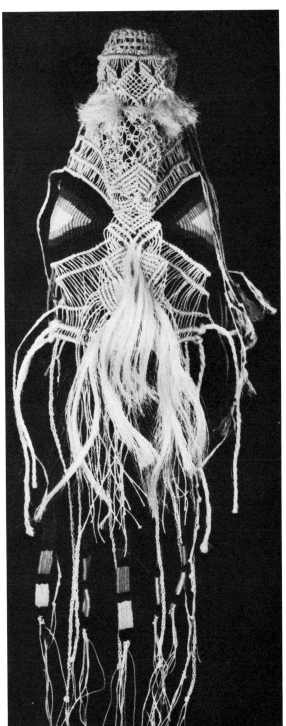

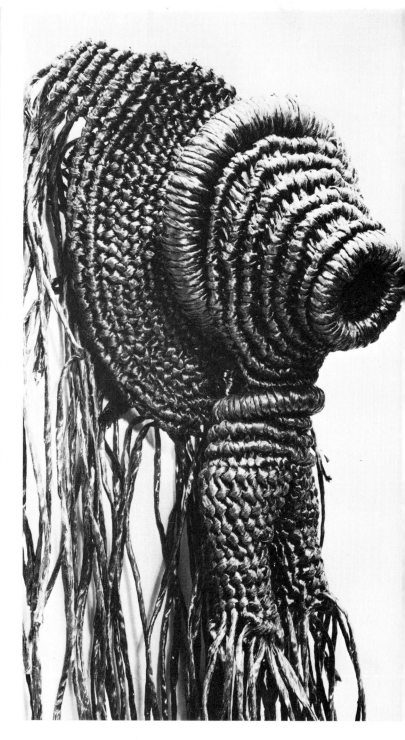

157 *(left)*   Mask, 120 cm × 25 cm
(3 ft 11 in. × 10 in.), Leslie Bohnenkamp.
Abstract mask evoking images of animal
mask or fetish. Mask has silvery cast from
the grey polypropylene, a man-made
straw-like fibre. *Collection of Jon Wahling*

158 *(right)*   Mask *(detail)*, Leslie
Bohnenkamp

Bibliography

Ashley, Clifford W, *The Ashley Book of Knots,* Faber and
    Faber, London; Doubleday, Garden City, New York,
    1944

Coats, J and P, *Anchor Manual of Needlework,* Batsford,
    London, 1958; Branford, Newton Centre

DeDillont, Thérèse, 'Macramé', in *Encyclopedia of Needle-
    work,* DMC Library, Mulhouse, France, pp 407–456

Harvey, Virginia I, *Color and Design in Macramé,* Van
    Nostrand Reinhold, London and New York, 1971

Harvey, Virginia I, *Macramé: The Art of Creative Knotting,*
    Van Nostrand Reinhold, London and New York,
    1967

Meilach, Dona, *Macramé: Creative Design in Knotting,*
    Crown, New York, 1971; George Allen and Unwin,
    London

Paque, Joan Michaels, *Visual Instructional Macramé,* Joan
    and Henry Paque, Milwaukee, Wisconsin, 1971

Pesch, Imelda Manalo, *Macramé Creative Knotting,* Sterling
    Publishing Co, New York, 1970; Oak Tree Press,
    London

Philips, Mary Walker, *Step by Step Macramé,* Golden Press,
    New York, 1970; Pan Books, London

Short, Eirian, *Introducing Macramé,* Batsford, London,
    1970; Watson-Guptill Publications, New York

Suppliers

In both Great Britain and the United States of America good stationers, garden suppliers, hardware stores, yachting and marine suppliers sell a variety of strings and ropes. Needlecraft as well as sewing departments of large stores stock threads of all kinds. Below is a list of specialist suppliers.

GREAT BRITAIN

Macramé threads and twines

E. J. Arnold Limited (School Suppliers), Butterley Street, Leeds LS10 1AX
Arthur Beale, 194 Shaftesbury Avenue, London WC2
British Twines Limited, 112 Green Lanes, London N16
Dryad Limited, Northgates, Leicester LE1 4OR
John Lewis Limited, Oxford Street, London W1
Mace and Nairn, 89 Crane Street, Salisbury, Wiltshire
M. Mallock and Sons, 44 Vauxhall Bridge Road, London SW1
The Needlewoman Shop, 146–148 Regent Street, London W1
Nottingham Handcraft Company (School Suppliers), Melton Road, West Bridgford, Nottingham

Beads

Bourne and Hollingsworth Limited, Oxford Street, London W1
Ells and Farrier Limited, 5 Princes Street, London W1

UNITED STATES

The following suppliers are mail order companies which send out catalogues and samples of their goods

Macramé threads and twines

Craft Yarns of Rhode Island, 603 Mineral Spring Avenue, Pawtucket, Rhode Island 02862
House of Harvey, 2724 NE 55th, Seattle, Washington 98105
Macramé and Weaving Supply Company, 63 East Adams Street, Chicago, Illinois 60603
P. C. Herwig Company, Square Knot Headquarters, 264 Clinton Street, Brooklyn, New York 11201

Beads

Earthbeads, 624 W. Willow Street, Chicago, Illinois 60614